Ketogenic Diet Cookbook Box Set:

3 Ketogenic Books in 1, Ketogenic Slow Cooker, Ketogenic Dump Dinners & Ketogenic Freezer Meals

Book 1: *Ketogenic Slow Cooker Recipes: Low Cab, Fix it and Forget it, Ketogenic Crock Pot Recipes*

Book 2: *Ketogenic Dump Diner Recipes: Quick and Easy Dump Dinners For Healthy Weight Loss*

Book 3: *Ketogenic Diet Freezer Meals: Keto Diet Make Ahead Freezer Mal Recipes For Quick Easy Meals & Ketogenic Diet Weight Loss*

By
Ashley Peters

clarifying purposes only and are the owned by the owners themselves, not affiliated with this document.

As a "Thank You" for purchasing this book, I want to give you a gift absolutely 100% Free

** Follow the instructions at the end of this book to receive Keto Holiday Recipes FREE **

Introduction

Congratulations and Thank You!

I want to start by thanking you for downloading the book, "Ketogenic Diet Cookbook Box Set: 3 Ketogenic Books in 1, Ketogenic Slow Cooker, Ketogenic Dump Dinners & Ketogenic Freezer Meals." I am honored to be helping you on this journey to create Paleo recipes!

With the Ketogenic Diet Box Set, you will be able to explore three types of cooking styles that fall completely within the guidelines of the Ketogenic diet: Slow cooker cooking, which simmers food on low heart cooking the contents inside; dump dinners, which are one-pot solutions to your favorite meals; and freezer meals, which allow you to make your meals ahead of time, freeze them, and then thaw them as needed throughout the week or month. This flexibility allows you to cook some amazing dishes for yourself and for your loved ones while maintaining the diet that you have found works for you. With the multitude of recipes and cooking styles, you will never grow bored with the Ketogenic diet!

What is the Ketogenic Diet? (Keto Diet)

Despite the many different kinds of diets that you have no doubt heard about in your life, there is bound to be a few that are new to you. One of these in particular might be the Ketogenic Diet, also known as the Keto Diet, which is a high-fat, low-carbohydrate regimen. The theory behind the high-fat, low-carbohydrate ratio is that the body will rely on fat for energy instead of on carbohydrates, and therefore the body will become more lean as a result of having less fat stored in the body. Ideally, the Keto Diet will allow the body to go into ketosis, or a metabolic state where ketones - which are fats - are burned for energy instead of glucose - the carbohydrates. Those that follow the Keto Diet also consume just the right amount of protein that the body needs on a daily basis. Contrary to some of the other diets that are in existence, the Keto Diet does not focus on counting calories. The focus is instead centered on the fat, carbohydrate, and protein make-up of the food as well as on the weight of the portions.

But what led to the creation of the Keto Diet? Back in 1924, a Mayo Clinic doctor by the name of Russell Wilder developed the Ketogenic Diet in hopes of finding a treatment for epilepsy. Many people who suffer from epilepsy and other illnesses have reported a noticeable decrease in their symptoms after going on this diet. This practice dates back to Ancient Greece when doctors would change their patients' diets and even have them fast to force their body into starvation mode. The Ketogenic Diet is a much easier means of getting the body to go into the fasting mode without actually depriving the body of food. To this day, however, no one knows exactly why the Ketogenic Diet is so effective in helping those that suffer from epilepsy, autism, and other known illnesses.

A typical meal for someone on the Ketogenic Diet would feature the high-fat, low-carbohydrate ratio, and might include a healthy serving of a protein such as chicken, some fruit or a protein-rich vegetable, and a high-fat component, which might be butter. The high-fat component on this diet usually comes from the ingredients which go into making the food; this could include heavy cream, butter, or buttermilk, and also might feature creamy dressings such as Ranch.

Why Choose the Ketogenic Diet?

Over the years, researchers have found that there are many benefits to choosing the Ketogenic Diet. There was initial speculation that the diet would cause a cholesterol build-up in the body, therefore leading to heart disease due to the high-fat content of the foods that people on the diet could consume. However, as more and more experts have looked into the diet, they have found that there are inherent advantages for beginning this type of diet. For one, the body is able to utilize fat instead of carbohydrates for energy. The body will therefore not rely on carbohydrates since there is such a low amount entering the body, and will thus be able to store ketones - the fats - for later energy use.

Another benefit is the fact that the body will not be as hungry, and people on the Keto Diet therefore are at a lower risk of falling off their regiment by snacking. Because the Keto Diet encourages the consumption of various protein-rich foods which work to curb hunger. The body goes into the state of ketosis - which is common among those who fast regularly - and therefore does not require a lot of food to keep it going. What better than to be on a healthy diet and not have constant hunger pangs?

Finally, the health benefits offered by the Keto Diet are remarkable. People who follow the Keto Diet completely eliminate starchy carbohydrates, such as breads and pastas, and substitute them with non-starch vegetables such as broccoli, asparagus, carrots, and many others. These kinds of vegetables are packed with vitamins and nutrients that support a healthy body, and are also much lower in calories. The Keto Diet, in addition to aiding those who suffer from illnesses such as epilepsy, is also recommended for cancer patients. As research has shown, cancer cells flourish in areas of the body where there is a lot of glucose, which is what carbohydrates become. If the body consumes less carbohydrates, there will therefore be less glucose, and subsequently the cancer cells will not be able to grow and thrive.

Benefits Of A Keto Diet

•Cholesterol. A Keto diet has shown to improve triglyceride levels and cholesterol levels most associated with arterial buildup.

•Weight Loss. As your body is burning fat as the main source of energy, you will essentially be using your fat stores as an energy source while in a fasting state.

•Blood Sugar. Many studies show the decrease of LDL cholesterol over time and have shown to eliminate ailments such as type 2 diabetes.

•Energy. By giving your body a better and more reliable energy source, you will feel more energized during the day. Fats are shown to be the most effective molecule to burn as fuel.

•Hunger. Fat is naturally more satisfying and ends up leaving us in a satiated ("full") state for longer.

•Acne. Recent studies have shown a drop in acne lesions and skin inflammation over 12 weeks.

Table of Contents

INTRODUCTION 5

WHAT IS THE KETOGENIC DIET? (KETO DIET) 5

WHY CHOOSE THE KETOGENIC DIET? 7

BENEFITS OF A KETO DIET 8

BOOK 1: KETOGENIC SLOW COOKER RECIPES 13

BENEFITS OF THE SLOW COOKER 13
SLOW COOKER TIPS & TRICKS 14
KETO SLOW COOKER THAI SOUP 16
KETO SLOW COOKER BACON OMELET 17
KETO SLOW COOKER CABBAGE TOMATO CHICKEN & SAUSAGE SOUP 18
KETO SLOW COOKER MEDITERRANEAN STEW 19
KETO SLOW COOKER FAT BURNING SOUP 20
KETO SLOW COOKER PORK STEW 21
KETO CHILI WITH A TWIST 22
KETO SLOW COOKER PORK HOCK 24
KETO SLOW COOKER BEEF & EGGPLANT CASSEROLE 25
KETO SLOW COOKER POACHED SALMON 26
KETO SLOW COOKER CHICKEN FAJITA SOUP 27
KETO SLOW COOKER LEMON CHICKEN 28
KETO SLOW COOKER SPICY LAMB 29
KETO SLOW COOKER LEMONGRASS PORK 31
KETO SLOW COOKER CHUCK STEAK 32
KETO SLOW COOKER TURKEY DRUMSTICKS 33
KETO SLOW COOKER PORK WITH APPLE & MUSTARD SAUCE 34
KETO SLOW COOKER CHICKEN WITH GARLIC CLOVES 35
KETO SLOW COOKER BEEF RAGS 36
KETO SLOW COOKER PULLED PORK 37
KETO SLOW COOKER SHREDDED BEEF WITH & HERBS 38
KETO SLOW COOKER BEEF SLICES 39
KETO SLOW COOKER MEATLOAF 40
KETO SLOW COOKER BREAKFAST CASSEROLE 41
KETO SLOW COOKER CHICKEN & GARLIC BUTTER 42
KETO SLOW COOKER STUFFED PEPPERS 43
KETO SOUTH OF THE BORDER CASSEROLE 44

KETO SLOW COOKER BBQ RIBS...45

KETO SLOW COOKER CHOCOLATE CAKE...46

KETO SLOW COOKER LIME & SALSA PORK CHOPS..............................47

KETO SLOW COOKER BEEF CHILI..48

KETO SLOW COOKER CHICKEN FAJITAS..49

KETO SLOW COOKER MEATBALLS...50

KETO SLOW COOKER BUFFALO CHICKEN...51

KETO SLOW COOKER PORK CARNITAS...52

KETO SLOW COOKER LIME CHICKEN...53

KETO SLOW COOKER CHEESE & MUSHROOM......................................54

KETO SLOW COOKER PEPPERONI BEEF...55

KETO SLOW COOKER MEXICAN CHICKEN..56

KETO SLOW COOKER BONE BROTH...57

KETO SLOW COOKER POT ROAST..58

KETO SLOW COOKER RADISH & PORK BELLY....................................59

KETO SLOW COOKER CHICKEN DRUMSTICKS....................................60

KETO SLOW COOKER ZUCCHINI NOODLES & CHICKEN...................61

KETO SLOW COOKER VEGGIE & BEEF STEW.......................................62

KETO SLOW COOKER MEXICAN SOUP..63

KETO SLOW COOKER ASIAN CHICKEN...65

KETO SLOW COOKER CHICK ROAST...66

KETO SLOW COOKER THYME CHICKEN..67

KETO SLOW COOKER TURKEY SMASH...68

KETO SLOW COOKER CREAMY MUSHROOM CHICKEN.....................69

KETO SLOW COOKER HAM..70

KETO SLOW COOKER BREAKFAST PIE...71

KETO SLOW COOKER SPICY LAMB..72

KETO SLOW COOKER BEEF CURRY...73

KETO SLOW COOKER SPICY STEAK..74

KETO SLOW COOKER PUMPKIN CAKE...75

KETO SLOW COOKER SEAFOOD SOUP...76

KETO SLOW COOKER PIZZA MEATLOAF..77

BOOK 2: KETOGENIC DUMP DINER RECIPES 78

WHAT ARE DUMP DINNERS?...78

KETOGENIC DUMP ZESTY FIESTA CHICKEN DINNER......................79

KETOGENIC DUMP PEANUT CHICKEN DINNER.................................80

KETOGENIC DUMP STICKY CHICKEN DINNER...................................81

KETOGENIC DUMP JERK CHICKEN DINNER...82

KETOGENIC DUMP LAMB SHANKS DINNER..83

KETOGENIC DUMP LEMON CHICKEN DINNER 84

KETOGENIC DUMP CHOCOLATE CHICKEN DINNER...85

KETOGENIC DUMP BEEF STEW DINNER...86

KETOGENIC DUMP MEATBALL SPAGHETTI SQUASH DINNER 87

KETOGENIC DUMP TURKEY CHILI DINNER...88

KETOGENIC DUMP HERB CARNITAS DINNER..89

KETOGENIC DUMP GREEK CHICKEN DINNER 90

KETOGENIC DUMP COFFEE BRISKET DINNER 91

KETOGENIC DUMP CORN CHOWDER DINNER..92

KETOGENIC DUMP TEXAS BEANS & BEEF DINNER 93

KETOGENIC DUMP SAUERKRAUT PORK DINNER 94

KETOGENIC DUMP PINEAPPLE CHICKEN DINNER 95

KETOGENIC DUMP CURRIED CHICKEN & VEGGIES DINNER..96

KETOGENIC DUMP JALAPENO BEEF DINNER...97

KETOGENIC DUMP ROASTED VEGGIE & TOMATO SOUP DINNER................................98

KETOGENIC DUMP MUSHROOM & CHICKEN DINNER 99

KETOGENIC DUMP WILD RICE & CHICKEN SOUP DINNER.......................................100

KETOGENIC DUMP PASTA WITH ITALIAN PORK CHOPS DINNER 101

KETOGENIC DUMP STEAK ROLL UP DINNER...102

KETOGENIC DUMP PORK DINNER...103

KETOGENIC DUMP ROASTED BEEF WITH MUSHROOMS DINNER..............................104

KETOGENIC DUMP VEAL STEW DINNER...105

KETOGENIC DUMP ITALIAN VEAL ROAST DINNER 106

KETOGENIC DUMP PEPPER BEEF STEAK DINNER 107

KETOGENIC DUMP ANAHEIM CHILE BEEF DINNER 108

KETOGENIC DUMP SHERRY BRAISED BEEF RIBS DINNER..109

KETOGENIC DUMP MUSTARD SHORT RIBS DINNER...110

KETOGENIC DUMP COFFEE ROASTED BEEF DINNER 111

KETOGENIC DUMP BBQ SPARE RIBS DINNER 112

KETOGENIC DUMP RUMP STEAK ITALIAN STYLE DINNER.......................................113

KETOGENIC DUMP BEER CHUCK ROAST DINNER 114

KETOGENIC DUMP SAUERKRAUT SPARE RIBS DINNER 115

KETOGENIC DUMP MONTPARNASSE BEEF STEAK DINNER.......................................116

KETOGENIC DUMP SHREDDED BEEF STEAK DINNER...117

KETOGENIC DUMP MARENGO VEAL STEW DINNER...118

KETOGENIC DUMP CHICKEN & POTATO SOUP DINNER.............................119
KETOGENIC DUMP CHICKEN & CORN CHOWDER DINNER..........................120
KETOGENIC DUMP SWEET & SOUR CHINESE CHICKEN DINNER.....................122
KETOGENIC DUMP GARLIC & BUTTER CHICKEN DINNER...........................123
KETOGENIC DUMP GINGERROOT CHICKEN DRUMSTICKS DINNER..................124
KETOGENIC DUMP SAUSAGE & CHICKEN STEW DINNER............................125

BOOK 3: KETOGENIC DIET FREEZER MEALS.................................... 126

FREEZER MEAL TIPS...126
KETOGENIC FREEZER COCONUT PEANUT CURRY SOUP.............................128
KETOGENIC FREEZER CHEESY BOUILLON REUBEN SOUP..........................129
KETOGENIC FREEZER BROCCOLI CHICKEN CHEESE SOUP.........................131
KETOGENIC FREEZER CREAMY CAULIFLOWER, BACON AND CHICKEN SOUP...........133
KETOGENIC FREEZER CREAMY CHICKEN.......................................135
KETOGENIC FREEZER EASY CHICKEN...136
KETOGENIC FREEZER AVOCADO BAKED CHICKEN................................137
KETOGENIC FREEZER CREAMY MUSHROOM SOUP.................................139
KETOGENIC FREEZER THAI BROCCOLI CHICKEN................................140
KETOGENIC FREEZER THAI GREEN CURRY CHICKEN.............................141
KETOGENIC FREEZER HEALTHY SOUP...143
KETOGENIC FREEZER TEX MEX SOUP...145
KETOGENIC FREEZER FRUITS & VEGGIES SOUP................................147
KETOGENIC FREEZER CHILI..149
KETOGENIC FREEZER CHICKEN BBQ PIZZA SOUP...............................151
KETOGENIC FREEZER BAKED AVOCADO CHICKEN................................153
KETOGENIC FREEZER CHEESY CHICKEN CASSEROLE.............................155
KETOGENIC FREEZER PORK WITH MUSHROOMS AND SOUR CREAM...................157
KETOGENIC FREEZER SHORT-RIB STEW.......................................159
KETOGENIC FREEZER BROCCOLI HAMBURGER CASSEROLE.........................161
KETOGENIC FREEZER STUFFED BEEF PEPPERS.................................163
KETOGENIC FREEZER CHEESY MEATLOAF......................................165
KETOGENIC FREEZER CHICKEN AND HERB PARMESAN............................167
KETOGENIC FREEZER CHICKEN WITH PEANUT CURRY SAUCE......................169
KETOGENIC FREEZER BAKED MEATBALLS......................................171
CONCLUSION...172
FREE GIFT - KETO HOLIDAY RECIPES.......................................173

Book 1: Ketogenic Slow Cooker Recipes

Benefits of the Slow Cooker

Whether you know it by the name "Crock Pot" or "slow cooker", you understand that the function of this invaluable tool is to help foodies and first-time cooks alike. In actuality, the name Slow Cooker refers to the brand, while a slow cooker is the generic name for the device. Since its inception, the Slow Cooker has helped countless people to become more confident in their cooking, while saving them time and money along the way. The Slow Cooker was first introduced to the world in the 1940s, and since that time kitchens around the world have never been the same. Essentially, a Slow Cooker is a vessel that is portable and heats its contents evenly, allowing a thorough cooking of the food that is inside. That, however, is not the only benefit of this device.

The time that a Slow Cooker can save you is a major advantage of stocking your kitchen with one. If you are unfamiliar with how to work one, it's really a very simple process: simply prepare the ingredients that you need according to the directions - so you can chop, slice, dice your ingredients beforehand. When you have finished, you place the ingredients in the pot, set it to the proper heat as well as the length of time, and walk away from your Slow Cooker. The only time you have to come back - aside from stirring, if needed - is when it is time to eat! Many people place their ingredients in the Slow Cooker and head off to work or to run errands if the heat is set to low. That way, they don't have to spend time over a stove, unable to break away from the kitchen.

Another benefit is that you save money when you buy and prepare food in bulk. Slow Cookers come in a variety of sizes, and many are very large vessels that can hold a ton of food for you and your family. If you are someone who likes to watch your wallet a bit, then the Slow Cooker is definitely something for you. Make double the amount that you need for you and your family, and then you can have leftovers for the next day's lunch or dinner. This is a huge cost-saving method, especially for families that have different financial obligations, and in the long run will be a great advantage.

Slow Cooker Tips & Tricks

All Slow Cooker experts know that there are a multitude of tips that are out there to help you maximize and better your experience with your Slow Cooker. For the best possible outcome when it comes to your slow cooked meals, your best bet is to get acclimated to the different tricks that you can rely on so that your food comes out tasting incredible every time.

One of the first tips that any expert will tell you is to purchase and use the right size vessel. If you are preparing a meal for only two people, you are not going to use a Slow Cooker that has a capacity to feed 15. You will either wind up making too much food and will be forced to throw some of it out, or the actual cooking process will suffer if you do not load the pot with the proper amount of food and/or liquid that is required.

Another tip is to make sure that you do not lift the lid too many times during the cooking process. Of course, you are going to want to stir your food, and if the recipe calls for that, then only do so when it says you should. Others are going to want to reasonably give the food a little whiff to inhale all of the aromas and goodness that is cooking in the pot. This is absolutely fine to do if you do not leave the lid off for too much time. You will lose precious heat that has built up inside, and your food will not cook as evenly when the heat off the top has managed to escape.

Finally, one of the best tips that you can follow is one that will be a tremendous health benefit to you. Never put frozen food - especially meats - in your Slow Cooker. Because of the low heat settings, you do not want bacteria to form when your food is slowly cooking throughout the day. Instead, make sure that only fresh ingredients are going into the Slow Cooker at all times to guarantee that you will not contribute to bacteria growth inside the vessel.

Follow these tips and tricks and your Slow Cooker experience will always be a positive one!

Keto Slow Cooker Thai Soup
Makes: 6 servings

INGREDIENTS:

2 tablespoons red curry paste
2 12 ounce cans of coconut milk
2 cups chicken stock
2 tablespoons fish sauce
2 tablespoons brown sugar
2 tablespoons peanut butter
1½ lbs. chicken breasts, cut into 1½ inch pieces
1 red bell pepper, seeded and sliced into ¼ inch slices
1 onion, thinly sliced
1 heaping tablespoon fresh ginger, minced
1 cup frozen peas, thawed
1 tablespoon lime juice
cilantro for garnish

INSTRUCTIONS:

•Mix together curry paste, coconut milk, chicken stock, fish sauce, brown sugar and peanut butter in a slow-cooker bowl.
•Add chicken breast, red bell pepper, onion and ginger to the slow cooker.
•Cook covered on high for 4 hours.
•Stir in the peas and cook for another ½ hour.
•Mix lime juice.
•Serve with cilantro

Keto Slow Cooker Bacon Omelet

Makes 1 serving

Each Serving - 463 Calories, 39g Fats, 1g Net Carbs, and 24g Protein.

INGREDIENTS:

2 slices Bacon, already cooked

1 tsp. Bacon Fat

2 large Eggs

1 oz. Cheddar Cheese

2 stalks Chives

Salt and Pepper to Taste

INSTRUCTIONS:

•Grate the cheese.

•Cook the bacon.

•Chop the chives.

•Heat the bacon fat in pan over medium-low heat.

•Add the beaten eggs.

•Season with chives, salt and pepper.

•When the edges being to set, add bacon to the center.

•Cook for 20-30 seconds.

•Turn off the heat.

•Sprinkle cheese over the bacon.

•Fold two edges of the omelet onto the cheese.

•Hold for a moment to hold them in place.

•Repeat with the other edges.

•Flip over and cook for a little longer.

Keto Slow Cooker Cabbage Tomato Chicken & Sausage Soup
Makes: 6-8 servings

INGREDIENTS:

6 cups chopped cabbage (1 lb.)
1 onion, chopped small
1 cup celery, diced small
2 cans (14.5 oz.) petite dice tomatoes
6 cups beef stock
2 tsp. dried thyme
1 tsp. ground fennel
fresh ground black pepper to taste
4 (or 6) links Sabatinos Chicken Sausage with Mozzarella, Artichokes and Garlic
2 tsp. olive oil
Freshly-grated Parmesan cheese for serving (optional)

INSTRUCTIONS:

•Chop cabbage, onion, and celery & put in the slow cooker
•Pour in the 2 cans of tomatoes, beef stock, dried thyme, ground fennel, and black •pepper to the slow cooker.
•Cook for 8-9 hours on low or 3-4 hours on high.
•Slice the sausage into ¼ inch pieces.
•Heat the olive oil over medium-high heat.
•Add sausage & cook until well browned.
•Stir in the sausage to the soup.
•Cook for 30-45 minutes on high.
•Serve with freshly-grated Parmesan cheese if desired.

Keto Slow Cooker Mediterranean Stew

Makes: 6 servings

INGREDIENTS:

1-2 tablespoons olive oil
8 oz. sliced mushrooms
1 onion, diced in 1/2 inch pieces
2 lbs. trimmed and diced chuck steak (in bite-sized pieces)
1 cup beef stock
1 can (14.5 oz.) diced tomatoes with juice
1/2 cup tomato sauce
1/4 cup balsamic vinegar
1 can black olives, cut in half
1/2 cup garlic cloves sliced thin
2 tablespoons finely chopped fresh rosemary
2 tablespoons finely chopped fresh parsley
1 tablespoon capers
Freshly ground black pepper & salt

INSTRUCTIONS:

•Heat small quantity of olive oil in frying pan.
•Sauté mushrooms until begins to brown.
•Add to slow cooker.
•Sauté diced onions in frying pan until starting to brown.
•Add to slow cooker.
•Brown diced beef for about 10-15 minutes.
•When done add beef to the slow cooker.
•Pour 1 cup beef stock to frying pan.
•Simmer until slightly reduced.
•Add to the slow cooker.
•Put in diced tomatoes & juice, tomato sauce, balsamic vinegar, olives, garlic, rosemary, •parsley, capers, and a little black pepper to the slow cooker.
•Stir gently to mix.

19

•Close lid & cook 6-8 hours on low.
•Season to taste & serve.

Keto Slow Cooker Fat Burning Soup
Makes: 20 servings

INGREDIENTS:

6 medium green onions
2 green peppers
1 can (14.5 oz.) petite diced tomatoes
1 cup crushed tomatoes
1 medium bunch celery (10 stalks)
4 cloves crushed garlic
1 small head cabbage
Salt & pepper
3 cubes beef bullion
2 teaspoons dried parsley
1 tablespoon dried onion flakes
1 teaspoon onion powder
½ teaspoon garlic powder
1/3 cup grated parmesan cheese (optional)

INSTRUCTIONS:

•Chop ingredients into pieces.
•Place in slow cooker except for cheese.
•Pour in water to cover vegetables.
•Close and cook on low for 5 hours.
•Season to taste & additional if desired.
•Stir in cheese.

Keto Slow Cooker Pork Stew

Makes: 4 servings

Each serving - 386 Calories, 28.9g Fats, 6.4g Net Carbs, 19.9g Protein.

INGREDIENTS:

1 lb. Cooked Pork Shoulder
2 tsp. Chili Powder
2 tsp. Cumin
1 tsp. Minced Garlic
1/2 tsp. Salt
1/2 tsp. Pepper
1 tsp. Paprika
1 tsp. Oregano
1/4 tsp. Cinnamon
2 Bay Leaves
6 oz. Button Mushrooms
1/2 sliced Jalapeno
1/2 medium Onion
1/2 Green Bell Pepper, sliced
1/2 Red Bell Pepper, sliced
Juice 1/2 Lime (to finish)
2 cups Gelatinous Bone Broth
2 cup Chicken Broth
1/2 cup Strong Coffee
1/4 cup Tomato Paste

INSTRUCTIONS:

•Wash and chop vegetables
•Heat 2 tbsp. Olive Oil over high heat.
•Add vegetables and sauté until slightly cooked.
•Slice pork into bite size chunks.
•Pour bone broth, chicken broth, and coffee in to slow cooker.
•Add pork and mushrooms and mix.
•Stir in spices & vegetables with the oil to the slow cooker.

•Mix, cover, & leave on low for 4-10 hours.
•When done open & stir.

Keto Chili with a Twist
Makes: 4 servings
Per serving: 398 Calories, 17.8g Fats, 5.3g Net Carbs, an 51.8g Protein.

INGREDIENTS:

2 lbs. Stew Meat
1 Medium Onion
1 Medium Green Pepper
1 Cup Beef Broth
1/3 Cup Tomato Paste
2 Tbsp. Soy Sauce
2 Tbsp. Olive Oil
2 Tbsp. + 1 tsp. Chili Powder
1 1/2 tsp. Cumin
2 tsp. Red Boat Fish Sauce
2 tsp. Minced Garlic
2 tsp. Paprika, 1 tsp. Oregano
1 tsp. Cayenne Pepper, 1 tsp. Worcestershire
1 tsp. Black Pepper, 1 tsp. Salt

INSTRUCTIONS:

•Cut half of the meat into small cubes.
•Make the other half into ground beef.
•Chop pepper and onion into small pieces.
•Mix together all spices together to make sauce.
•Heat olive oil in a pan.
•Add beef and brown cubed and ground & transfer to a slow cooker.
•Use remaining fat in the pan to sauté onions until translucent and also the veggies.

•Place in the slow cooker and mix together.
•Simmer on high for 2 1/2 hours.
•Open & simmer for 20-30 minutes.

Keto Slow Cooker Pork Hock

Makes: 2 servings

Per serving: 520 Calories, 29g Fat, 8g Net Carbs, and 22g Protein.

INGREDIENTS:

1 lb. Pork Hock
1/4 Cup Rice Vinegar
1/3 Cup Soy Sauce
1/3 Cup Shaoxing Cooking Wine
1/4 Cup Splenda
1/3 Medium Onion
1 Tbsp. Butter (Coconut Oil can also be used)
Handful of Shitake Mushrooms
1 tsp. Chinese Five-Spice
1 tsp. Oregano
2 Cloves Garlic, Crushed

INSTRUCTIONS:

•Fry the onions up.
•Boil shitake mushrooms.
•Begin to sear the pork hock in butter until skin starts to turn crispy.
•Put all the ingredients in to the slow cooker.
•Mix well. (rice vinegar, soy sauce, five-spice, oregano, cooking wine, Splenda, onion, mushrooms, garlic, and onion).
•Cook for 2 hours on high heat.
•Stir and cook for another 2 hours on low heat.
•Remove the pork hock from the slow cooker and de-bone.
•Cut as desired and put it back to the slow cooker.
•Serve with steamed vegetables & sauce.

Keto Slow Cooker Beef & Eggplant Casserole

Makes servings: 12

Per serving: 209 calories, 12.8g fat, 733mg sodium, 8.1g carbs, 2.4g fiber, 5.7g net carbs, 15.9g protein

INGREDIENTS:

2 cups eggplant, cubed

A dash of salt

1 tablespoon olive oil

2 lbs. ground beef

2 teaspoons salt

1/2 tsp. pepper

2 tsp. Worcestershire sauce

2 tsp. mustard

28 oz. canned tomatoes, drained

16 oz. canned tomato sauce

2 cups mozzarella cheese, grated

2 Tablespoons parsley

1 tsp. oregano

INSTRUCTIONS:

•Sprinkle eggplant with salt & leave in a colander for about 30 minutes.

•Place in bowl and stir in olive oil.

•Mix ground beef, salt, pepper, Worcestershire sauce and mustard together.

•Place in slow cooker and press on bottom and sides.

•Add eggplant.

•Put in tomatoes and sauce over eggplant.

•Sprinkle with remaining ingredients.

•Cook for 3-4 hours on slow and 2-3 hours on high.

Keto Slow Cooker Poached Salmon

Makes: 4 to 6 servings
Per serving: Calories520, Fat 30.5 g (46.9%), Saturated 6.9 g (34.6%),
Carbs 1.9 g (0.6%)
Fiber 0.2 g (0.8%), Sugars 0.6 g, Protein 46.5 g (93%), Cholesterol
124.7 mg (41.6%)
Sodium 723 mg (30.1%

INGREDIENTS:

2 cups water
1 cup dry white wine
1 lemon, thinly sliced
1 shallot, thinly sliced
1 bay leaf
5-6 sprigs fresh herbs, such as tarragon, dill, and/or Italian
parsley
1 teaspoon black peppercorns
1 teaspoon kosher salt
2 lbs. skin-on salmon (or 4-6 fillets), preferably farm-raised
Kosher salt and freshly ground black pepper
Lemon wedges, coarse sea salt, and olive oil for serving

INSTRUCTIONS:

•Mix together water, wine, lemon, shallots, bay leaf, herbs,
peppercorns &salt in slow cooker.
•Cook for 30 minutes on high.
•Season salmon with salt and pepper.
•Pace in the slow cooker with skin side down.
•Cover & cook on low until salmon flakes gently with a fork.
•Check after 45 minutes whether done.
•Sprinkle with good-quality olive oil & coarse salt.
•Serve with wedges of lemon.

Keto Slow Cooker Chicken Fajita Soup

Makes: 14 servings

Per Serving: Calories: 73, Carbs: 4 net grams, Fat: 1.5 g, Protein: 12 g

INGREDIENTS:

1 ½ lb. Chicken Breast

32 oz. Chicken Stock

14.5 oz. Can Diced Tomatoes

1 Medium Yellow Bell Pepper – Diced

1 Medium Orange Bell Pepper – Diced

1 Medium Onion Diced

6 oz. Mushrooms Sliced thin

4 Large Cloves Garlic minced

4 Tbs. Taco Seasoning

2 Tbs. Fresh Cilantro chopped

1 Tbs. Garlic Salt

INSTRUCTIONS:

•Heat slow cooker on low setting.

•Put all the ingredients in to slow cooker.

•Cover & cook for 6 hours on low.

•Shred the chicken breasts with forks.

•Cover & cook for another 1 hour.

Keto Slow Cooker Lemon Chicken
Makes: 6 to 8 servings

INGREDIENTS:

2 carrots, chopped
2 ribs celery, chopped
1 bulb fennel, cored and chopped
1 onion, chopped
16 large stuffed green olives
4 cloves garlic, crushed
2 bay leaves
½ tsp. dried oregano
¼ tsp. salt
¼ tsp. pepper
12 boneless skinless chicken thighs
¾ cup sodium-reduced chicken broth
¼ cup all-purpose flour
2 tbsp. lemon juice
½ cup chopped fresh parsley
Grated zest of 1 Lemon

INSTRUCTIONS:

•Mix carrots, celery, fennel, onion, olives, garlic, bay leaves, oregano, salt & pepper together.
•Place in slow cooker.
•Add chicken over the vegetables.
•Pour in broth and ¾ cup water.
•Cover and cook for 5 ½ to 6 hours on low until juices run clear when chicken is pierced.
•Discard bay leaves.
•Mix until smooth flour with 1 cup of the cooking liquid.
•Stir in lemon juice and then into slow cooker.
•Cover and cook on high until thick, about 15 minutes.
•Mix parsley with lemon zest.

•Sprinkle over chicken.

Keto Slow Cooker Spicy Lamb
Makes: 4 servings
Per serving: Carbs 7.5 grams, Fiber 1.4 grams, Net Carbs 6.1 grams,
Protein 46.5 grams
Fat 38.4 grams, Saturated 18.3 grams, Energy 574 kcal, Potassium
976 mg

INGREDIENTS:

1 lamb leg, whole (4 lbs.)
¼ cup balsamic vinegar (2 fl oz.)
¼ cup strawberry vinegar or any sugar free fruit vinegar (2 fl oz.)
4 cloves black aged garlic (or fresh white garlic)
1-2 sprigs fresh rosemary
4 heads small lettuce (14.2 oz.)
½ tsp. salt or to taste
2-3 cups water

INSTRUCTIONS:

•Preheat the oven to 300 F.
•Peel & slice the garlic into smaller pieces.
•Place the lamb leg in a baking dish.
•Season with salt & add water.
•Add balsamic vinegar, fruit vinegar, sliced garlic and rosemary.
•Cover with a lid.
•Cook in the oven for about 2 hours.
•The timing is 30 minutes for every 1 lb. of lamb leg.
•Open lid after 2 hours & increase the temperature to 400 F.
•Cook for another 30-45 minutes.
•Remove from the oven and leave to cool.
•Shred meat with a fork while warm.
•Pour sauce over the shredded meat.
•Separate & wash the lettuce leaves.

•Tap off the excess water with paper towel.
•Top with the shredded meat mixture.

Keto Slow Cooker Lemongrass Pork
Makes: 6 – 8 servings

INGREDIENTS:

2-3 lbs. Pork Loin or Butt Roast
2 inch ginger
2-3 cloves garlic
2 tsp. kosher salt
3 TBS olive oil
3 TBS minced lemongrass
1 TBS apple cider vinegar
1 tsp. ground pepper
1 onion
½ can coconut milk

INSTRUCTIONS:

•Trim off any excess fat from the roast,
•Leave just a little.
•Slice a crisscross pattern into top fatty layer of the pork.
•Peel & mince the garlic.
•Peel & slice ginger into ¼ inch thick slices.
•Slice onion into ¼ inch rounds
•Put the onion rounds at the bottom of the slow cooker.
•Mix into a loose paste the olive oil, salt, minced garlic, minced lemongrass, apple cider vinegar, ground pepper.
•Apply the paste over the pork & place in slow cooker.
•Marinate covered, over night.
•Add ½ can of coconut milk to slow cooker the next day.
•Cook on low for 8 hours.
•When done, pork should fall apart.
•Shred with fork and serve!

Keto Slow Cooker Chuck Steak

Makes: 8 servings

INGREDIENTS:

2kg (4.4lbs) Chuck Steak
3 Carrots
4 Celery Stalks
1 Cup of Red Wine
2 Cloves of Garlic
2 Cups of Beef Stock
Salt and Pepper to taste
Herbs of your choice

INSTRUCTIONS:

•Heat large frying pan.
•Place beef in and let it caramelize – 5 minutes per side.
•Make 2 cups of beef stock.
•After beef is seared place in slow cooker.
•Pour red wine into the pan, and stir to deglaze.
•When the wine starts to simmer, add the some stock and stir for a few moments.
•Pour the remaining stock & deglaze mix from the pan, into slow cooker.
•Season with salt, pepper, garlic, herbs & a knob or two of butter.
•Close with lid & place on low heat.
•Wash & cut up carrots & celery into chunky pieces.
•Add to the meat and cook in all for about 6 hours.
•Check hourly.
•If necessary, top up the stock.

Keto Slow Cooker Turkey Drumsticks

Makes: 4 servings

INGREDIENTS:

1 tablespoon olive oil

3 turkey drumsticks

Sprinkles salt and cracked black pepper, to taste

1 large Vidalia onion, chopped

3 large carrots, peeled and sliced into thin coins

2 large cloves garlic, minced

½ teaspoon dried sage, crumbled

2 tablespoons fresh parsley, chopped

1 tablespoon fresh thyme, chopped (or use 1 teaspoon dried)

1 lemon, halved

INSTRUCTIONS:

•Oil the bottom of the slow cooker with olive oil.

•Rub the drumsticks with olive oil.

•Season well with salt and pepper.

•Arrange the onions and carrots in the bottom of the cooker.

•Place the drumsticks over.

•Mix garlic, sage, parsley & thyme together.

•Sprinkle over the drumsticks.

•Squeeze the lemon halves gently to release juices into the vegetables.

•Let them nestle at the bottom of the pot

•Cook for 8-10 hours on low, or high for 4-5 hours until meat is cooked through.

Keto Slow Cooker Pork with Apple & Mustard Sauce

Makes: 4 servings

INGREDIENTS:

2 lbs. pork shoulder joint
salt
1 cooking apple
4 ozs. chicken/vegetable stock
½ tsp. Dijon mustard
½ tsp. English mustard
1 tsp. cumin/cinnamon

INSTRUCTIONS:

Apple sauce
•Core and peel the apple & chop it up.
•Put it in a bowl & sprinkle with a teaspoon of stevia, & a pinch of cumin r cinnamon.
•Add a few teaspoons of water and cover with cling film.
•Microwave for 2 minutes.
•Stir & repeat until the sauce is formed.
•Mix in mustard with the apple sauce.
•Stir the apple/mustard sauce with the stock.
•Trim the fat off the pork & place on a clean surface.
•Make a few slits in the pork to let all the juices in.
•Sprinkle salt and rub it in.
•Place pork in slow cooker
•Pour the apple / mustard sauce over.
•Cook on high for two hours.
•Turn heat to low and cook for another 4-8 hours.
•Remove the pork and slice as desired.
•Pour sauce over.

Keto Slow Cooker Chicken with Garlic Cloves
Makes: 2 – 4 servings

INGREDIENTS:

1 whole chicken, rinsed and patted dry
(giblets and excess fat pockets removed)
Sprigs of fresh marjoram, sage, rosemary, and thyme; or
1 small bunch of fresh thyme
½ a lemon
About 40 cloves of garlic
Salt, pepper, paprika, or seasonings preferred

INSTRUCTIONS:

•Separate the garlic cloves & leave them unpeeled.
•Put the garlic cloves in the bottom of the slow cooker.
•Arrange the chicken on top, breast side up.
•Stuff the chicken cavity with the lemon.
•Season well with salt, pepper, and paprika and/or other seasonings
•Strip the leaves off of the herbs.
•Tear them and put on and around the chicken.
•Cook for 8 hours on low.
•When done separate the chicken into individual pieces.
•Broil on a baking sheet for a couple of minutes until skin is crisp.
•Serve with the garlic cloves.

Keto Slow Cooker Beef Rags

Makes: 6 servings
Per serving: 386 Calories; 14g Fat (37.4% calories from fat); 52g Protein; 3g Carbohydrate; trace Dietary Fiber; 80mg Cholesterol; 3g Effective Carbs

INGREDIENTS:

3 lbs. chuck arm pot roast
2 teaspoons granulated garlic
1 teaspoon onion powder
1/2 tablespoon kosher salt
1/2 tablespoon fresh ground black pepper
2 tablespoons Worcestershire Sauce
1 cup cabernet sauvignon—or dry red wine (screw-top is fine)
1/2 tablespoon Country Dijon Mustard
3 tablespoons unfiltered extra virgin olive oil

INSTRUCTIONS:

•Season the meat with granulated garlic, onion powder, kosher or coarse sea salt and freshly ground black pepper.
•Pour ½ of the olive oil in a heavy Dutch oven over medium high heat.
•Put in the meat & brown on all sides.
•Add remaining olive oil half way while browning.
•When meat is done sprinkle the top with Dijon mustard and Worcestershire Sauce.
•Pour in dry red wine.
•Place in slow cooker, cover & cook for 4-5 hours on medium.
•Check after 3 hours.
•If not fork tender replace lid and cook longer until fork tender.
•Remove from cooker.
•Shred meat into rags with forks.
•When shredding is done, stir it into the pan juices to mix well.

Keto Slow Cooker Pulled Pork

Makes: 12 servings
Per serving: Calories: 265, Fat: 16 g, Net Carbs: 1 g, Protein: 20 g,

INGREDIENTS:

3 Lbs. Boneless Pork Shoulder
2 tsp. Onion Powder
2 tsp. Garlic Powder
2 tsp. Salt
1 tsp. Black Pepper
1 tsp. Paprika
1 tsp. Ground Allspice
1 tsp. Celery Salt
1 tsp. Mustard Powder
1/2 cup Water

INSTRUCTIONS:

•Cut it off the bone to fit into slow cooker.
•Mix together onion powder, salt, pepper, garlic powder, paprika, allspice, celery salt, & mustard powder.
•Rub the mixture well into the meat on both sides.
•Pour water into the pork.
•Cook for 6 hours on high or 10 hours on low.
•When done, mash up the pork into pieces.
•Serve with sauce.

Keto Slow Cooker Shredded Beef with & Herbs

Makes: 6 – 8 servings

INGREDIENTS:

3 lbs. chuck roast
1 tablespoons sea salt
2 tsp. black pepper
1 yellow onion, sliced
3 cloves garlic, finely chopped
1 tsp. turmeric
1 tsp. cayenne pepper
3 sprigs fresh rosemary
2 sprigs fresh thyme
1/2 cup bone broth

INSTRUCTIONS:

•Rinse chuck roast in cold water.
•Pat dry with paper towels & leave aside.
•Mix salt, black pepper, turmeric, cayenne and chopped garlic.
•Add sliced onions and bone broth to slow cooker.
•Set to high.
•Coat the chuck roast evenly with spice mixture and place in slow cooker.
•Tie herbs in a bundle and place in cooker.
•Cook for 8 hours turning over after 4 hours
•Take out bundle of herbs.
•Shred beef with a fork.

Keto Slow Cooker Beef Slices

Makes: 4 servings

INGREDIENTS:

2 lb. chuck roast
juice of 1 orange
juice of 2 limes
1/4 cup extra virgin olive oil
¼ cup fresh minced cilantro
1 tsp. red pepper flakes
4 cloves garlic, minced
1 tsp. coconut sugar (optional)
½ tsp. coriander
2 tsp. oregano
¼ tsp. cumin
2 tsp. sea salt
1 large shallot, chopped

INSTRUCTIONS:

•Rinse beef under cold water.
•Dry & set aside for 30 minutes.
•Pulse all remaining ingredients in a food processor to combine.
•Put beef in slow cooker and coat well with Asada marinade.
•Stir in ¼ cup of filtered water.
•Cook for 5 hours on high, turning meat over every hour
•When done, remove meat & leave to rest for about 20 minutes.
•Slice meat across the grain.
•Spoon juices over & serve.

Keto Slow Cooker Meatloaf
Makes: 4 servings

INGREDIENTS:

Olive oil in a spritzer bottle, or non-stick cooking spray
2 lbs. extra lean ground sirloin
2 large eggs
1 cup (about 1 medium size) zucchini, grated and excess liquid squeezed out
1/2 cup freshly grated Parmesan cheese
1/2 cup fresh parsley, finely chopped, plus extra for garnish
4 cloves freshly minced garlic
3 Tablespoons balsamic vinegar
1 Tablespoon dried oregano
2 Tablespoons minced dry onion or onion powder
1/2 teaspoon sea or Kosher salt
1/2 teaspoon ground black pepper

TOPPING
1/4 cup ketchup or tomato sauce
1/4 cup shredded or 2-3 slices mozzarella cheese
2 Tablespoons fresh parsley chopped

INSTRUCTIONS:

•Line a large slow cooker with strips of aluminum foil.
•Spray with olive oil or non-stick cooking spray.
•Mix all ingredients except for cooking spray & topping ingredients.
•Pour mixture into the slow cooker.
•Shape into shaped of loaf a top of the aluminum foil strips.
•Put lid on top of slow cooker.
•Cook for 3 hours on high.
•Turn off the cooker 15 minutes before the end of cooking time.
•Take off lid

•Drizzle ketchup over the top of meatloaf.
•Top with cheese & replace the lid of slow cooker.
•Leave for 5-10 minutes until cheese melts.
•Transfer to serving platter & garnish with fresh parsley.

Keto Slow Cooker Breakfast Casserole
Makes: 6 – 8 servings
Per serving: Carbs 5.39 g, Fiber 1.18 g

INGREDIENTS:

1 medium head broccoli, chopped
1 12-oz package Jones Dairy Farm Little Links, cooked and sliced
1 cup shredded Cheddar, divided
10 eggs
3/4 cup whipping cream
2 cloves garlic, minced
1/2 tsp. salt
1/4 tsp. pepper

INSTRUCTIONS:

•Grease the ceramic interior of a slow cooker well.
•Place a layer of broccoli, sausage & cheese into the slow cooker.
•Repeat with remaining broccoli, sausage and cheese.
•Whisk well together eggs, whipping cream, garlic, salt and pepper.
•Pour over ingredients in slow cooker.
•Cover & cook for 4 to 5 hours on low or for 2 to 3 hours on high.
•Edges should be brown & center firm.

Keto Slow Cooker Chicken & Garlic Butter

Makes: 4 – 6 servings

INGREDIENTS:

For the garlic chicken
2- 2.5 lbs. of chicken breasts
1 stick of butter
8 garlic cloves, sliced in half to release flavor
1.5 tsp. salt
Optional -- 1 sliced onion
<u>Cheese sauce</u>
8 oz. of cream cheese
1 cup of chicken stock (I use the liquid left in the slow cooker after the chicken is removed.)
salt to taste

INSTRUCTIONS:

•Place the chicken in slow cooker.
•Put in the butter.
•Add the garlic spreading it around evenly.
•Sprinkle salt.
•Cover & cook on low for 6 hours.
•When done take out & place on serving platter.

Cheese sauce
•Pour cup of chicken stock into a pan (or liquid from the slow cooker).
•Stir in the cream cheese and salt.
•Cook until sauce is well blended & creamy over low medium heat.
•When done, pour over chicken.

Keto Slow Cooker Stuffed Peppers

Makes: 1 serving

Per Serving: Carbs: 9.4 Net Carbs: 7.0, Calories: 322, Fat: 9.6ngredients

INGREDIENTS:

1 poblano pepper

1/3 cup finely chopped cauliflower

1/3 lb. ground beef

1 tablespoon chopped onion

3 tablespoons tomato sauce

INSTRUCTIONS:

•Cut the pepper in half & remove seeds.

•Set aside.

•Brown together the ground beef and onion.

•Mix beef mixture with the cauliflower and tomato sauce.

•Spoon mixture into the pepper halves.

•Pour in 1/2 inch of water or tomato juice to the bottom of a slow cooker.

•Lay the stuffed peppers in carefully.

•Cook for about 4 hours on low, or until done.

Keto South of the Border Casserole

Makes: 10 servings

Per Serving: Calories: 320, Fat: 24.1g, Saturated fat: 10.8g,
Carbohydrates: 5.2g

Sugar: 1.6g, Sodium: 749mg, Fiber: .8g, Protein: 17.9g, Cholesterol:
231mg

INGREDIENTS:

12 oz. Pork Sausage Roll
1/2 teaspoon garlic powder
1/2 teaspoon coriander
1 teaspoon cumin
1 teaspoon chili powder
1/4 teaspoon salt
1/4 teaspoon pepper
1 cup salsa
10 eggs
1 cup milk, (I used 1%)
1 cup Pepper Jack cheese or cheese of choice
Optional toppings: sour cream. Avocado, salsa, cilantro

INSTRUCTIONS:

• Cook sausage until no longer pink over medium heat.
• Add seasonings and salsa.
• Leave to cool slightly.
• Whisk separately the eggs and milk.
• Fold in the sausage to the eggs.
• Add cheese and stir.
• Grease the bottom of slow cooker & pour in the mixture.
• Cover and cook for 2 1/2 hours on high or for 5 hours on low.

Keto Slow Cooker BBQ Ribs

Makes: 1 serving

Per serving: Calories: 775, Protein: 89g, Carbs: 14g, Fiber: 3g, Net Carbs: 11g, Fat: 39g

INGREDIENTS:

1 lb. Fresh Pork Ribs

1 ½ oz. Tomato Puree

¼ cup water

1/8 cup Vinegar

2 Tablespoons Worcestershire Sauce

1 Tablespoon Dry Mustard

1 Tablespoon Chili Powder

2 Tablespoons Splenda

INSTRUCTIONS:

•Coat a frying pan with calorie free cooking spray.

•Place on a high heat and add the ribs

•Brown both sides of ribs.

•Coat the bottom & sides of slow cooker with calorie free cooking spray.

•Place the ribs in slow cooker

•Mix the remaining ingredients until a consistent mixture is formed

•Pour over the ribs evenly as possible to cover.

•Coat ribs thoroughly & turn them.

•Slow cook for 8 hours on low.

Keto Slow Cooker Chocolate Cake
Makes: 10 servings
Per serving: 11.65 g of carbs and 5.38 g of fiber

INGREDIENTS:

1 & 1/2 cups almond flour

3/4 cup Swerve Sweetener

2/3 cup cocoa powder

1/4 cup unflavored whey protein powder

2 tsp. baking powder

1/4 tsp. salt

1/2 cup butter, melted

4 large eggs

3/4 cup almond or coconut milk, unsweetened

1 tsp. vanilla extract

1/2 cup Sugar-Free Chocolate Chips (optional)

INSTRUCTIONS:

•Grease a slow cooker well.

•Whisk almond flour, sweetener, cocoa powder, whey protein powder, baking powder and salt together.

•Fold in butter, eggs, almond milk and vanilla extract & mix well.

•Add chocolate chips.

•Pour mixture into slow cooker.

•Cook for 2 1/2 to 3 hours on low.

•Turn off heat.

•Leave to cool for 20 to 30 minutes.

Keto Slow Cooker Lime & Salsa Pork Chops

Makes: 1 serving

Calories 406, Protein: 57g, Carbs: 10g, Net Carbs: 8g, Fat: 16g

INGREDIENTS:

2 x Pork Loins
3 oz. Salsa
3 tablespoons Lime Juice
½ tsp. Ground Cumin
½ tsp. Garlic Powder
½ tsp. Salt
½ tsp. Ground Black Pepper
Calorie Free Cooking Spray

INSTRUCTIONS:

•Trim off the fat from pork chops.
•Mix the cumin, garlic powder, salt and pepper together.
•Rub the spice mixture well in to both sides of the pork chops.
•Coat a frying pan with calorie free cooking spray.
•Place the chops in pan & fry each side for 5 minutes over a medium heat.
•Spray the insides of slow cooker with the calorie free cooking spray
•Place pork chops in slow cooker.
•Pour the salsa and lime mixture over.
•Slow cook for 8 hours on low.
•When done place the pork chops on a plate.
•Garnish with salsa & lime mixture.

Keto Slow Cooker Beef Chili

Makes: 8 servings Per serving: Calories: 326 Fat: 17 Carbohydrates: 10 Sugar: 4

Fiber: 2 Protein: 23

INGREDIENTS:

2 lbs. grass-fed ground beef

2 - 15 ounce cans no sugar added tomato sauce

1 small 6 ounce can no sugar added tomato paste

5 Tablespoons chili powder

2 Tablespoons cumin powder

¼ cup dried onion flakes (or 1 medium onion chopped)

1 teaspoon garlic powder (or 2 cloves minced)

1 teaspoon Tabasco sauce

2 teaspoons fine ground Celtic sea salt

1 T dried or powdered oregano

Chicken or beef broth (for thinning)

INSTRUCTIONS:

•Brown the hamburger & onion.

•Chop very small

•If grass-fed beef no need to drain the fat.

•Add the onion flakes (if using), garlic, chili powder, cumin, oregano, salt, tomato paste when hamburger is almost done.

•Cook with tomato paste and spices until the hamburger is done.

•Stir in tomato sauce and Tabasco & cook for a few minutes.

•Place in slow cooker & cook for 1 – 2 hours until sauce is thick.

•Add broth if sauce is too thick.

Keto Slow Cooker Chicken Fajitas

Makes: 4 servings

INGREDIENTS:

1 1/2 lb. boneless, skinless chicken breasts
1 large white onion chopped
1 Tbsp. chopped garlic
1 tsp. dried oregano
1 tsp. chili powder
1 tsp. ground cumin
1/2 tsp. ground coriander
1/2 tsp. kosher salt
1/2 tsp. cayenne pepper
1 can of rotel

Additional Ingredient Options:
Low carb tortillas
Guacamole
Sour Cream
Shredded Cheese
Anything else you like on your fajitas

INSTRUCTIONS:

•Place all the ingredients in the slow cooker.
•Cook for 4 – 5 hours on high.
•Slice chicken into strips.
•Serve sliced chicken, onion/tomato mix, cheese, sour cream, guacamole on tortilla.

49

Keto Slow Cooker Meatballs
Makes: 4 servings

INGREDIENTS:

1 1/2 to 2 lbs. ground beef
1 medium onion
4 cloves garlic
2 large eggs
1 tablespoon almond flour (a substitute for traditional breadcrumbs)
Spices as desired - cayenne pepper, salt and pepper, dash of steak rub
Olive oil for browning in pan and to grease slow cooker

INSTRUCTIONS:

•Mince garlic & chop up onion.
•Mix vegetables & all other ingredients together.
•Shape meat into balls as preferred.
•Brown meatballs lightly over medium-high heat in olive oil greased pan.
•Place meatballs in greased slow cooker.
•Cook for 7 hours on low.

Keto Slow Cooker Buffalo Chicken

Makes: 6 servings
Calories 297, Fat: 8, Carbohydrates: 1, Fiber: 0, Protein: 52

INGREDIENTS:

6 Frozen Chicken Breasts
1 Bottle Frank's Red Hot
½ Packet Hidden Valley Ranch
3 Tablespoon Butter

INSTRUCTIONS:

•Put chicken in the slow cooker.
•Pour hot sauce over chicken and sprinkle ranch over top.
•Cover and cook for 6 hours on low.
•Shred the chicken.
•Add butter, and cook on low for 1 hour uncovered

Keto Slow Cooker Pork Carnitas

Makes: 16 servings

Per serving: Calories: 265, Fat: 9, Carbohydrates: 0, Fiber: 0, Protein: 8

INGREDIENTS:

8 lbs. Boston Pork Butt

2 Tablespoon Bacon Grease (use butter if necessary)

1 Large Onion

2 Tablespoon Cumin

2 Tablespoon Thyme

2 Tablespoon Chili Powder

1 Tablespoon Salt

1 Tablespoon Pepper

4 Tablespoon Minced Garlic

1 Cup Water

INSTRUCTIONS:

•Grease slow cooker.

•Line the bottom of slow cooker with sliced onion.

•Lay garlic over the onions.

•Trim off most of fat from the meat.

•Make cuts in a crisscross pattern into the top of the fat left on.

•Mix spices together and rub into meat into the cuts on fat.

•Sprinkle any leftover spices over onions and garlic.

•Place meat in slow cooker & add 1 cup of water.

•Cover & cook for 8 hours on high.

•When done the meat should completely fall apart.

Keto Slow Cooker Lime Chicken

Makes: 1 serving

INGREDIENTS:

24-oz. jar medium salsa
Juice from one lime
1/4 cup fresh cilantro, chopped
1.25-oz. package taco seasoning
2 jalapeños peppers, finely chopped (optional)
6 boneless chicken breast halves

INSTRUCTIONS:

•Mix together salsa, lime juice, cilantro, taco seasoning and jalapenos in slow cooker.
•Put in the chicken and coat with the salsa mixture.
•Cook covered, for 6 hours on low setting.
•Spoon salsa mixture over top.

Keto Slow Cooker Cheese & Mushroom

Makes: 4 servings

INGREDIENTS:

2 (8 ounce) fresh mushrooms

½ cup butter, melted

1 ounce ranch dressing mix (hidden valley, 1 package)

2 tablespoons parmesan cheese, as much as desired

INSTRUCTION:

•Put mushrooms in the slow cooker.

•Add Ranch dressing to melted butter in a bowl.

•Mix and pour over mushrooms.

•Sprinkle with Parmesan Cheese.

•Cook for 4 hours on low.

Keto Slow Cooker Pepperoni Beef

Makes: 6 servings

INGREDIENTS:

2 lbs. beef chuck roast
1 (16-ounce) jar pepperoncini peppers
optional:
6 oz. sliced mozzarella or Swiss cheese
6 hamburger buns or French rolls

INSTRUCTIONS:

•Place all the ingredients in the slow cooker.
•Set to low and cook for 8 hours.
•Shred the meat with large forks and stir.
•Serve with cheese on toasted bread, rolls, or buns.

Keto Slow Cooker Mexican Chicken

Makes: 4 – 6 servings

INGREDIENTS:

4 boneless, skinless chicken breasts
1 1/4 teaspoon cumin
1 tablespoon chili powder
1/2 teaspoon coriander
1/4 teaspoon paprika
1 1/2 teaspoon salt
1/2 tsp. black pepper
1/3 cup chicken broth
1/3 cup (packed) cilantro leaves, chopped
2 limes
1 large onion, chopped
1 jalapeno, seeded and minced
4 garlic cloves, minced
1 tablespoon olive oil

INSTRUCTIONS:

•Heat the oil in sauté pan.
•Stir in onion and sauté for 5 minutes.
•Add cumin, chili powder, coriander, paprika and garlic and sauté two more minutes. •Pour in chicken broth to deglaze pan.
•Turn off heat and set aside.
•Season chicken with salt and pepper.
•Place in slow cooker.
•Squeeze the lime over & add cilantro, jalapeno.
•Pour the onion and garlic mixture over.
•Close & cook on low for 3-5 hours.
•When done remove chicken breasts, shred and place in a bowl.
•Spoon the onions over the chicken.
•Pour any juice from slow cooker over the shredded chicken.

Keto Slow Cooker Bone Broth

Makes: 6 – 8 servings

INGREDIENTS:

5 lbs. marrow bones, ideally with some meat still on them
1/4 cup Apple Cider Vinegar
Filtered Water
2 Bay Leaves, optional

INSTRUCTIONS:

•Brown the bones for 30 minutes, turning them once or twice in an oven at 350 F.
•Place in the slow cooker & pour filtered water to cover.
•Add the Vinegar and Bay Leaves (if using).
•Cook for 24 hours on low.
•Stock should barely simmer.
•If too hot, adjust lid to cool.
•Scoop out marrow from each bone when cool with a knife.

Keto Slow Cooker Pot Roast
Makes: 6 – 8 servings

INGREDIENTS:

5 lb. pot roast
Himalayan Salt (or similar)
2 tablespoons tallow or lard
3 cups bone broth

INSTRUCTIONS:

•Salt the Roast generously.
•Heat the fat on medium-high heat.
•Brown the roast on all sides .
•Place in the slow cooker.
•Deglaze pan with the bone broth.
•Pour over the roast.
•Cook for 7-8 hours on low.

Keto Slow Cooker Radish & Pork Belly

Makes: 2 – 3 servings

INGREDIENTS:

1 lb. Pork Belly
1 teaspoon Himalayan Salt (or similar)
2 bunches radishes

INSTRUCTIONS:

•Slice Pork Belly into strips thicker-than-bacon.
•Place in the bottom of slow cooker.
•Sprinkle with salt.
•Close & place on low.
•Cook for 8-9 hours.
•Turn to high & trim the radishes.
•Cut in halves & quarters.
•Add to the slow cooker & stir.
•Cover & cook for another 40 minutes.
•Could be served with cold raw sauerkraut or sliced cucumber.

Keto Slow Cooker Chicken Drumsticks

Makes: 12 servings

Per serving: 587 calories, 42.8g fat, 640mg sodium, 0.7g carb, 53.5g protein

INGREDIENTS:

1/2 cup liquid aminos (or gluten free soy sauce)
2 cups water
1 teaspoon ground ginger
1 teaspoon garlic powder
2 tablespoons sweetener
1/4 teaspoon blackstrap molasses (optional)
6 1/2 lbs. chicken, cut into pieces
Salt and pepper

INSTRUCTIONS:

•Mix together soy aminos, water, ground ginger, garlic powder, sweetener, and molasses in slow cooker.
•Season chicken with salt and pepper.
•Add chicken to slow cooker.
•Cook for 5 – 6 hours on high.

Keto Slow Cooker Zucchini Noodles & Chicken
Makes: 4 servings

INGREDIENTS:

7 bone-in chicken thighs (about 3.5 lbs.), skin discarded
Salt and pepper
3/4 cup chopped scallions (about 6)
5 cloves garlic, chopped
1/4 cup soy sauce
¼ cup erythritol
1 teaspoon dried ginger
1/4 teaspoon sesame oil
6 medium zucchinis

INSTRUCTIONS:

•Grease slow cooker.
•Remove chicken skin.
•Season both sides with salt and pepper & place in slow cooker.
•Mix together ¾ of the chopped scallions, chopped garlic, soy sauce, erythritol, ginger, and sesame oil.
•Pour over chicken in slow cooker.
•Cook on low for 4 hours.
•Cut off the ends from each zucchini.
•Follow the instructions on Vegetti package to turn into noodles, using thick side.
•Lightly press noodles over the chicken 15 minutes before cooking ends.
•Close the slow cooker.
•Lightly mix together.
•Sprinkle with remaining scallions.

Keto Slow Cooker Veggie & Beef Stew
Makes: 8 servings

INGREDIENTS:

2.5 lbs. stew meat
1/3 cup almond flour
½ teaspoon salt
½ teaspoon black pepper
3 cloves garlic
2 bay leaves
1 teaspoon paprika
8 sprigs of thyme
¼ cup fresh parsley, chopped
1 teaspoon Worcestershire sauce
1 onion, chopped
2 cups beef broth
8 oz. mushrooms, sliced
2 green peppers, chopped
3 stalks celery, chopped
10 oz. frozen spinach

INSTRUCTIONS:

•Place the meat in slow cooker.
•Mix together almond flour, salt and black pepper.
•Pour over meat and stir to coat.
•Sauté mushrooms in olive oil.
•Mix the bay leaves, paprika, thyme, parsley, Worcestershire sauce, onion, beef broth, mushrooms, peppers, and celery together.
•Spoon this mixture into slow cooker and mix well.
•Close & cook on high for 6 hours or low for 10 hours.
•Add spinach (not thawed), to the mixture 30 minutes before cooking time is up.

•Cover with gravy.
•When cooking is done, remove thyme & bay leaves.
•Add salt and pepper to taste.

Keto Slow Cooker Mexican Soup
Makes: 5 – 6 servings
Per serving: Calories 330, carbs 9, fiber 1.2, net carbs 8.2, protein 30, fat 18.

INGREDIENTS:

3 tbsps. butter (or oil)
1.5 medium onions- chopped
3 cloves garlic
1/2 big leek – chopped
1 big zucchini – chopped into small pieces
Red and green peppers, finely chopped - optional
1 can tomatoes – diced
(optional if you can have the extra carbs – 1 small jar salsa (watch for added sugar)
1 small (the tiny ones) can tomato purée
1 chicken stock cube
1 vegetable stock cube
10 cups Water
1 teaspoon sea salt
1/2 teaspoon black pepper
1/2 teaspoon white pepper
1/2 teaspoon cayenne pepper
1/2 teaspoon chili powder
1/2 teaspoon cumin powder
1.5 lbs. chicken thighs, boneless
7 oz. cream cheese
For each bowl of soup

1 tbsp. Sour cream

3 tbsps. shredded cheese

INSTRUCTIONS:

•Melt butter over medium heat.

•Stir in onions, garlic, leek and zucchini.

•Stir for a few minutes until soft. Do not brown.

•Pour in canned tomatoes and tomato purée & stir.

•Add water, stock cubes and spices.

•Pour into slow cooker & cook on low for 1 hour.

•Wash and chop into bite size pieces.

•Add chicken to slow cooker cook for 1 hour.

•Stir in the cream cheese.

•Season as desired.

•Serve with a handful of shredded cheese & dollop of sour cream.

Keto Slow Cooker Asian Chicken

Makes: 6 servings

Per serving: 392 calories, 23g fat, 3.5g net carbs, 37g protein

INGREDIENTS:

For the chicken:

6 chicken thighs

1 Tbsp. Chinese Five Spice Powder see example

1/2 tsp. kosher salt

For the sauce

1 cup no sugar added mandarin orange slices see example

1 tsp. minced garlic

1 Tbsp. minced ginger

1/2 tsp. sliced red chilis (or red pepper flakes)

1 Tbsp. lime juice

1 Tbsp. granulated sugar substitute

1 tsp. sesame oil

2 Tbsp. fish sauce

INSTRUCTIONS:

•Rub the chicken spice powder and salt.

•Sear each side for 3 minutes with skin side down over high heat.

•Place chicken with skin side up in slow cooker.

•Mix all sauce ingredients together.

•Pour over the chicken.

•Cook for 4 hours on high.

•Place chicken on a serving dish.

•Pour sauce over the chicken.

•Garnish with cilantro (optional).

Keto Slow Cooker Chick Roast

Makes: 4 – 6 servings

INGREDIENTS:

3-4 lb. beef chuck roast
2 cups beef stock
2 tbsp. red wine vinegar
2 tbsp. Worcestershire sauce
¼ cup soy sauce
1 tbsp. tomato paste
1 tbsp. liquid smoke
1 tsp. garlic powder
1 tsp. onion powder
Provolone cheese (optional)
Salt and pepper to taste

INSTRUCTIONS:

•Mix all of the ingredients together.
•Place in slow cooker.
•Lastly add the chuck roast.
•Cook on high for 4 hours

Keto Slow Cooker Thyme Chicken
Makes: 4 servings

INGREDIENTS:

1 large whole chicken
Rub Chicken
2-3 tbsp. ghee
1 tsp. Himalayan salt
1 tsp. freshly cracked black pepper
1 tbsp. fresh thyme, finely chopped
zest of 1 lemon
1 clove garlic, minced
Stuff Chicken
1 whole lemon, washed and cut into quarters
3-4 cloves garlic, peeled and smashed
3-4 sprigs fresh thyme
Bed for the Chicken
1 leek, washed and chopped
1 lemon, washed cut in half (use the one you zested)
6 garlic cloves, peeled and smashed
7-8 sprigs fresh thyme
Generous sprinkle of salt and pepper

INSTRUCTIONS:

•Mix all the ingredients listed under "rub".
•Remove the skin from chicken.
•Delicately run fingers under from butt end.
•Between the skin and meat, starting with the breasts.
•Gently, carefully, move all the way to front and under, and over legs too.
•Separate the skin from the meat.
•Do not tear the skin.
•Apply about ¾ of the rub directly on meat, under loosened skin.

•Any leftover rub to be applied on the skin, from outside.
•Stuff chicken with lemon wedges, garlic & fresh thyme.
•Tie up the legs with butcher's twine.
•Place chopped leek, garlic and fresh thyme at bottom of slow cooker.
•
•Add lemon halves at both ends & place chicken over.
•Sprinkle salt and pepper, place refrigerator for 2 hours to marinade.
•Cook for 5 hours on high.

Keto Slow Cooker Turkey Smash
Makes: 4 servings

INGREDIENTS:

1 small onion
1 each, orange, red, yellow bell peppers
2 green bell peppers
1 lb. ground turkey
Salt & pepper to taste
Oregano
Garlic powder

INSTRUCTIONS:

•Chop up onion & bell peppers.
•Place in slow cooker.
•Crumble turkey and add to the slow cooker.
•Stir in the seasoning & mix well.
•Cook for 2 – 3 hours on low until done.

Keto Slow Cooker Creamy Mushroom Ch

Makes: 8 servings
Per Serving: Calories: 493.6, Total Fat: 30.2 g, Cholesterol: 138
Sodium: 829.6 mg
Total Carbs: 4.5 g, Dietary Fiber: 0.2 g, Protein: 50.0 g

INGREDIENTS:

3 lbs. raw boneless, skinless chicken breast, cut in large chunks
2 cups fresh mushrooms, sliced
1 (8 oz.) bottle Ken's Steak House Creamy Caesar Dressing
4 oz. Neufchatel cheese (low-fat cream cheese)
1 can (10.75 oz.) cream of chicken soup
8 oz. part skim mozzarella cheese, shredded

INSTRUCTIONS:

•Pour Caesar dressing into slow cooker.
•Add chicken and mushrooms.
•Stir to coat.
•Cook on high for about 4 1/2 hours.
•Mix the cream of chicken soup and softened cream cheese together.
•Stir gently into slow cooker.
•Gently add in the cheese.
•Cook for another 1/2 hour until cheese melts.

Keto Slow Cooker Ham
Makes: 2 – 3 servings

INGREDIENTS:

1.5kg Ham
55 ml cider vinegar or red wine vinegar
10g artificial sweetener.
1 tablespoon water
1/2 teaspoon brown sugar (optional)
1 1/2 tablespoon German Mustard

INSTRUCTIONS:

•Mix 6g of the artificial sweetener or a 1/3 of the honey with the water.
•Pour into the bottom of slow cooker.
•Mix together the sweetener, vinegar, brown sugar and mustard separately.
•Coat the meat sides of the ham with the mustard mix.
•Do not cover the fat with the mixture.
•Place the ham into the slow cooker.
•Cook for around 7 hours at the lowest temperature.
•When done, remove & leave aside for about 15 minutes.
•Slice & serve.

Keto Slow Cooker Breakfast Pie

Makes: 4 – 6 servings

INGREDIENTS:

8 eggs, whisked

1 sweet potato or yam, shredded

1lb US Wellness Meats Pork Sausage, broken up

1 yellow onion, diced

1 tablespoon garlic powder

2 teaspoons dried basil

salt and pepper, to taste

any extra veggies

INSTRUCTIONS:

•Grease slow cooker with coconut oil.

•Add all ingredients to slow cooker.

•Mix well.

•Cook on low for 6-8 hours.

•Slice it like a pie.

Keto Slow Cooker Spicy Lamb

Makes: 4 servings

Per serving: Total Carbs 7.5 grams, Fiber 1 4 grams, Net Carbs 6.1 grams

Protein 46.5 grams, Fat 38 4 grams, Energy 574 kcal, Potassium 976 mg

INGREDIENTS:

1 lamb leg, whole (4.5 lbs.)
¼ cup balsamic vinegar
¼ cup strawberry vinegar
4 cloves black aged garlic (or fresh white garlic)
1-2 sprigs fresh rosemary
4 heads small lettuce
½ tsp. salt or to taste
2-3 cups water

INSTRUCTIONS:

•Peel & slice the garlic into small pieces.
•Place lamb in slow cooker.
•Add balsamic vinegar, fruit vinegar, sliced garlic and rosemary.
•Season with salt and add water.
•Cover & cook on high for about 2 – 3 hours.
•When done, leave to cool down for a few minutes.
•Shred meat while warm.
•Pour sauce over the shredded meat.
•Separate the lettuce leaves & wash.
•Leave for excess water to drain.
•Spoon with the shredded meat mixture.

Keto Slow Cooker Beef Curry

Makes: 6 servings

INGREDIENTS:

1 ½ lbs. beef suitable for stewing/casserole cut into large pieces

8 oz. coconut cream

1 red onion quartered

1 tsp. ground cardamom

1 tsp. Chinese five spice

½ tsp. chili powder

1 tsp. ground cinnamon

4 cloves garlic

2 tsp. ground coriander

1 tsp. ground cumin

1 tsp. turmeric

large handful of leafy greens

INSTRUCTIONS:

•Put coconut cream and all the spices into the slow cooker & mix.

•Stir in chopped onion and chopped beef, mix.

•Cook for 4-6 hours on high.

•Fold in gently the greens to slow cooker 5 minutes prior to serving.

Keto Slow Cooker Spicy Steak

Makes: 6 servings

Per Serving: Carbs: Carbs: 5.8 Net carbs: 4.0, Calories: 358, Fat: 13.8Ingredients

INGREDIENTS:

A couple of twists of ground pepper (roughly a teaspoon)

1/2 teaspoon Kosher salt

2-1/2 lbs. boneless round steak

1 14-1/2 oz. can Ro Tel tomatoes

1 tablespoon liquid smoke, mesquite flavor

1-1/3 cups beef broth

1 cup sliced celery

1/2 cup sliced onions

1/2 cup sliced carrots

1/2 cup bell pepper

2 peeled and minced garlic cloves

INSTRUCTIONS:

•Add all of the ingredients to the slow cooker.

•Cook covered for 8 to 10 hours on low.

Keto Slow Cooker Pumpkin Cake

Makes: 10 servings
Per serving: Carbs 10.03 g, and 5.61 g of fiber.

INGREDIENTS:

1 1/2 cups raw pecans
3/4 cup Swerve Sweetener
1/3 cup coconut flour
1/4 cup un-flavored whey protein powder
2 tsp. baking powder
1 1/2 tsp. ground cinnamon
1 tsp. ground ginger
1/4 tsp. ground cloves
1/4 tsp. salt
1 cup pumpkin puree
4 large eggs
1/4 cup butter, melted
1 tsp. vanilla extract

INSTRUCTIONS:

•Grease slow cooker or line with parchment paper.
•Grind the pecans until they resemble coarse meal (do not turn them into butter) in food processor.
•Place in a bowl.
•Stir in sweetener, coconut flour, whey protein powder, baking powder, cinnamon, ginger, cloves and salt.
•Blend in pumpkin puree, eggs, butter and vanilla until well combined.
•Pour into prepared slow cooker.
•Set to low & cook for 2 1/2 to 3 hours.
•Until set and top is barely firm to the touch.

Keto Slow Cooker Seafood Soup
Makes: 8 – 10 servings

INGREDIENTS:

4 (6 1/2 oz.) cans minced clams with juice
1/2 lb. salt pork or bacon, diced
1 cup chopped onion
6 to 8 medium potatoes, peeled and cubed
3 cups water
3 1/2 teaspoons salt
1/4 teaspoon pepper
4 cups half and half cream or milk
3 to 4 tbsp. cornstarch
chopped fresh parsley, for garnish

INSTRUCTIONS:

•Chop clams into bite-sized pieces if necessary.
•Sauté salt pork or bacon and onion until golden brown & drain.
•Place in slow cooker with clams.
•Put in all remaining ingredients, except milk, cornstarch, and parsley.
•Cover and cook on high 3 to 4 hours until vegetables are tender.
•Mix 1 cup of milk or cream with the cornstarch
•Stir in cornstarch mixture and the remaining milk or cream during last hour of cooking..
•Top each serving with chopped parsley.
•Serve with crackers or crusty French bread

Keto Slow Cooker Pizza Meatloaf
Makes: 8 servings

INGREDIENTS:

1 14 oz. jar pizza sauce (divided)
1 beaten egg
1/4 cup chopped onion
1/2 cup chopped green pepper
1/3 cup dry bread crumbs
1/2 tsp. Italian seasoning
1/2 tbsp. minced garlic
1/3 cup shaved Parmesan
1/4 tsp. black pepper
1 lb. ground beef
1/2 lb. hot pork sausage
1 cup shredded mozzarella
Diced fresh parsley for garnish (optional)

INSTRUCTIONS:

•Lay 3 strips of aluminum foil into the slow cooker.
•Reserve 1/2 cup of pizza sauce.
•Mix together 2/3 cup pizza sauce and the egg.
•Add onion, green pepper, bread crumbs, Italian seasoning, garlic, Parmesan, and black pepper.
•Stir in ground beef and pork sausage.
•Mix with hands.
•Shape into a loaf and place into slow cooker on top of aluminum foil strips.
•Cover and cook 4 to 6 hours on high.
•Layer loaf with the reserved 1/2 cup of pizza sauce and mozzarella cheese.
•Cover and cook for 15 minutes or until cheese is melted.

Book 2: Ketogenic Dump Diner Recipes

What are Dump Dinners?

When you think about the phrase "dump dinner", there are a few things that might come to mind. Those who have never cooked or even heard of a dump dinner may not know what to think! If you have ever heard of a dump cake - one in which all the ingredients are just dumped into the baking mold and then put into the oven without any mixing or blending - then you have very nearly cracked the idea of a dump dinner. The theory behind this phenomenon is ease and speed: people who are low on time and energy, yet want to create delicious meals for their families, are sometimes unable to accomplish their culinary desires. Due to their busy schedules, they resort to something quick and easy, perhaps even take-out. This can get costly, however, and in the end is not the best option in keeping the family healthy. Dump Dinners are the solution because you can create quick, easy, healthy meals with little effort.

Ketogenic Dump Zesty Fiesta Chicken Dinner
(Servings: 4)

INGREDIENTS:

1 lb. skinless chicken breasts

1 large white onion, sliced

2 red bell peppers, seeded and julienned

2 green bell peppers, seeded and julienned

1 yellow bell pepper, seeded and julienned

2 jalapeno peppers, seeded and sliced

4 garlic cloves, minced

1 cup medium cheddar cheese, shredded

1 tsp. oregano

1 tsp. paprika

1 tsp. cumin

1 tsp. salt

1 tsp. black pepper

2 tbsp. olive oil

INSTRUCTIONS:

•Dump all the ingredients in a slow cooker except the cheddar cheese.

•Cook covered for 8 hours on low.

•Add the cheddar cheese during the final half hour of cooking.

Ketogenic Dump Peanut Chicken Dinner
(Servings: 4)

INGREDIENTS:

1 lb. bones, skinless chicken breasts, cubed
¼ cup organic peanut butter
3 tbsp. soy sauce
1 cup filtered water
1 tsp. salt
2 tsp. red chili pepper flakes
Olive oil

INSTRUCTIONS:

•Grease the slow cooker with olive oil.
•Dump all the ingredients in a slow cooker.
•Cook for 8 hours on low.

Ketogenic Dump Sticky Chicken Dinner

INGREDIENTS:

1 1/2 lbs. chicken tenders, fresh
3 tbsp. no sugar ketchup
3 tbsp. natural peanut butter
1 tbsp. soy sauce

INSTRUCTIONS:

•Marinate the chicken with the sauces and butter for 4 hours.
•Dump the chicken in a baking dish.
•Bake for 20-30 minutes at 350F.

Ketogenic Dump Jerk Chicken Dinner
(Servings: 4-6)

INGREDIENTS:

8 scallions, chopped coarse
1/4 cup vegetable oil
2 habanero chilies, stemmed and seeded
1 (1-inch) fresh ginger, peeled and sliced 1/4 inch thick
2 tbsp. molasses
3 garlic cloves, peeled
1 tbsp. thyme
2 tsp. allspice
1/4 tsp. cardamom
1 tsp. coarse salt
4 lbs. bone-in, skin-on chicken pieces (split breasts, thighs)
Lime wedges for serving

INSTRUCTIONS:

•Puree the scallions, oil, allspice, habaneros, ginger, thyme, garlic, molasses, salt and cardamom in a blender and transfer half cup mixture into the slow cooker, reserving the rest.
•Dump the chicken into the slow cooker and coat with the pureed mixture.
•Cook for 4-6 hours on low.
•Transfer the chicken to a wire rack and brush it with the reserved puree.
•Broil the chicken until crisp and charred for 10 minutes, flip and then repeat.
•Serve with the lime wedges.

Ketogenic Dump Lamb Shanks Dinner

INGREDIENTS:

4 (1 1/2-lb.) lamb shanks, fat trimmed

1 (19-oz.) can cannellini beans or other white beans, rinsed and drained

1 1/2 cups diced peeled carrot

1 cup chopped onion

3/4 cup chopped celery

2 garlic cloves, thinly sliced

2 tsp. dried tarragon

1/2 tsp. salt

1/4 tsp. freshly ground black pepper

1 (28-oz.) can diced tomatoes, undrained

INSTRUCTIONS:

•Dump the beans, carrot, onion, celery and garlic in an electric slow cooker, mixing well and place the lamb shanks on top.

•Sprinkle the salt, pepper and tarragon and pour over the tomatoes.

•Cook covered on high for an hour and then reduce the heat to low.

•Cook for 9 hours.

•Transfer the lamb shanks into a plate, remove the lamb meat and discard the bones.

•Serve the lamb with the bean mixture.

Ketogenic Dump Lemon Chicken Dinner
(Servings: 6-8)

INGREDIENTS:

2 carrots, chopped
2 ribs celery, chopped
1 bulb fennel, cored and chopped
1 onion, chopped
16 large stuffed green olives
4 cloves garlic, crushed
2 bay leaves
½ tsp. dried oregano
¼ tsp. salt
¼ tsp. pepper
12 boneless skinless chicken thighs
¾ cup sodium-reduced chicken broth
¾ cup water
¼ cup all-purpose flour
2 tbsp. lemon juice
½ cup chopped fresh parsley
Grated zest of 1 Lemon

INSTRUCTIONS:

•Dump the carrots, fennel, onion, celery, garlic, olives, oregano, bay leaves, salt and pepper in a slow cooker and place the chicken pieces on top.
•Pour in the broth and water and cook for 5 ½ -6 hours covered until when the chicken is pierced, the juices run clear.
•Whisk together the flour with the lemon juice and 1 cup cooking liquid and then pour into the slow cooker.
•Cook covered on high for 15 minutes.
•Serve garnished with lemon zest and parsley.

Ketogenic Dump Chocolate Chicken Dinner
(Servings: 6)

INGREDIENTS:

2 lbs. chicken pieces (breasts and legs work well) bone in, Skin removed
Salt and pepper
2 tbsp. ghee
1 medium onion, chopped and sautéed
4 cloves garlic, crushed and sautéed
6 - 7 whole tomatoes, peeled, seeded and chopped
5 dried New Mexico chili peppers, rehydrated and chopped
¼ cup almond butter
2.5 oz. dark chocolate (70% or above)
1 tsp. sea salt
1 tsp. cumin powder
½ tsp. cinnamon powder
½ tsp. guajillpo chili powder
Avocado, cilantro and jalapeno, all chopped for garnish

INSTRUCTIONS:

•Season the chicken with salt and pepper and brown the chicken in ghee.
•Dump the chicken with the rest of the ingredients except the garnish ingredients in the slow cooker.
•Cook for 4-6 hours on low.
•Garnish with the avocado, cilantro and jalapeno.

Ketogenic Dump Beef Stew Dinner

INGREDIENTS:

2 lbs. Stew Beef

3 tbsp. Olive Oil

2 cups Organic Beef Stock

12 oz. Package Bacon, Cooked Crisp and Crumbled

14.5 oz. Can Organic Diced Tomatoes, Juice Drained

4 oz. Mixed Bell Peppers, Chopped

4 oz. Mushrooms, Quartered

2 Ribs Celery, Chopped

1 Large Carrot, Chopped

1 Small Onion, Chopped

4 Large Cloves Garlic, Minced

2 tbsp. Organic Tomato Paste

2 tbsp. Worcestershire Sauce

2 tsp. Sea Salt

1 ½ tsp. Black Pepper

1 tsp. Garlic Powder

1 tsp. Onion Powder

1 tsp. Dried Oregano

INSTRUCTIONS:

•Brown the beef in olive oil in a skillet and transfer into a slow cooker.

•Dump the rest of the ingredients in the slow cooker.

•Cook covered for 6-8 hours on low.

Ketogenic Dump Meatball Spaghetti Squash Dinner

INGREDIENTS:

One medium spaghetti squash, halved and seeds scooped out
One lb. of ground Italian sausage, shaped into meatballs
One (14-oz.) can of tomato sauce
2 tbsp. of hot pepper relish
4 to 6 cloves of garlic, whole
2 tbsp. of olive oil
2 tsp. Italian seasoning (Oregano, Basil, Thyme) to taste

INSTRUCTIONS:

•Dump the olive oil, tomato sauce, hot pepper relish, garlic and Italian seasoning in a slow cooker and stir mix.
•Place the squash halves face down in the slow cooker, surrounded by the meatballs.
•Cook covered for 5 hours on low.
•Pull the squash into spaghetti using a fork and place on a platter, topping with the meatballs.

Ketogenic Dump Turkey Chili Dinner
(Servings: 8-10)

INGREDIENTS:

2 lbs. of ground turkey

1 onion, diced and sautéed

3 cloves of garlic, minced and sautéed

1 red and 1 green bell pepper, both diced

1 cup of carrots, finely diced

1 cup of celery, diced

1 jalapeno, minced

1 (28-oz.) can of stewed tomatoes

1 (14-oz.) can of diced tomatoes

1 (15-oz.) can of tomato sauce

3 tbsp. of chili powder

1 tbsp. of oregano

1 tbsp. of basil

2 tsp. of cumin

1 tsp. of salt

1 tsp. pepper

1 tsp. onion powder

1/2 tsp. of cayenne

4 strips cooked bacon, crumbled

INSTRUCTIONS:

•Brown the ground turkey in a skillet and transfer to a Slow Cooker.

•Dump the rest of the ingredients except bacon into the Slow Cooker and stir mix.

•Cook covered for 6 hours on low.

•Garnish with crumbled bacon.

Ketogenic Dump Herb Carnitas Dinner

INGREDIENTS:

3.5 lb. pork roast
Sea salt and pepper
Olive oil
1 tbsp. dried thyme
4 bay leaves
1 cup chicken broth

INSTRUCTIONS:

•Season the pork roast with salt and pepper and brown the roast in olive oil in a skillet.
•Dump the roast in the Slow Cooker along with the rest of the ingredients.
•Cook covered for 6 hours on low.
•Shred the roast.

Ketogenic Dump Greek Chicken Dinner
(Servings: 6)

INGREDIENTS:

2 lbs. boneless skinless chicken breast
3 cups finely chopped spinach
2 roasted red peppers, chopped
1/4 cup sliced black olives
1 cup chopped artichoke hearts
4 oz. reduced fat feta
1 tbsp. oregano, chopped
1 tsp. garlic powder
1.5 cups chicken broth
Salt and pepper

INSTRUCTIONS:

•Combine the roasted red peppers, spinach, artichoke hearts, oregano, feta and garlic in a bowl.
•Season the chicken with salt and pepper and create pockets in the chicken using a knife.
•Stuff the chicken with the spinach mixture and dump the chicken breasts into the pressure cooker and pour in the broth.
•Cook for 4 hours on low.

Ketogenic Dump Coffee Brisket Dinner
(Servings: 8)

INGREDIENTS:

2 tbsp. packed brown sugar

1 tbsp. ground coffee

1 tbsp. paprika

1 tsp. garlic powder

1 tsp. ground black pepper

1 tsp. salt

1 (3 – lb.) boneless beef brisket, chopped to fit into cooker

2 large onion, sliced

1/2 cup strong brewed coffee

1 tbsp. balsamic vinegar

INSTRUCTIONS:

•Combine the ground coffee, brown sugar, garlic powder, paprika, salt and pepper in a bowl and season the brisket with the mixture.

•Dump the meat into the slow cooker and cover with the onion slices.

•Mix the vinegar and brewed coffee and pour over.

•Cook covered for 9-10 hours on low.

•Slice the meat across the grain and serve with the cooked onions.

Ketogenic Dump Corn Chowder Dinner
(Servings: 6)

INGREDIENTS:

3/4 cup dry yellow split peas

2 (14 1/2 – oz.) cans reduced-sodium chicken broth

1 cup water

1 (12 – oz.) package frozen corn kernels

1/2 cup chopped bottled roasted red sweet peppers

1 (4 – oz.) can diced green chiles

1 tsp. ground cumin

1/2 tsp. dried oregano, crushed

1/2 tsp. dried thyme, crushed

1/2 cup tub-style cream cheese spread with chive and onion

INSTRUCTIONS:

•Dump all the ingredients in a slow cooker except the cream cheese spread.

•Cook covered for 5-6 hours.

•Place two cups of the soup in a blender and puree and return back to the cooker.

•Whisk the cream cheese into the soup and cook covered for 5 minutes.

Ketogenic Dump Texas Beans & Beef Dinner
(Servings: 8)

INGREDIENTS:

1 (2 1/2 - 3 – lb.) boneless arm chuck roast, fat trimmed

2 tsp. chili powder

1 tsp. ground cumin

1 tsp. dried oregano, crushed

1/2 tsp. garlic powder

1 medium onion, cut into wedges

1 (15 – oz.) can pinto beans, drained and rinsed

1 (14 1/2 – oz.) can diced tomatoes, drained

1 (4 – oz.) can diced green chiles

1/3 cup chipotle barbecue sauce

INSTRUCTIONS:

•Season the roast with the chili powder, oregano, cumin and garlic powder and dump in the slow cooker with the rest of the ingredients other than the barbeque sauce.

•Cook covered for 8-10 hours on low.

•Remove the roast, chop into eight pieces and return to the cooker.

•Mix in the BBQ sauce and cook for 5 minutes on high.

Ketogenic Dump Sauerkraut Pork Dinner
(Servings: 8)

INGREDIENTS:

1 1/2 lbs. tiny red new potatoes, quartered

1 (14 3/4 – oz.) can sauerkraut with caraway seeds, rinsed and drained

1 tbsp. packed brown sugar

2 lbs. boneless pork shoulder, chopped into 1 ½ inch pieces, discard excess fat

2 tbsp. stone ground mustard

1/2 tsp. ground black pepper

1 cup beer

1/4 cup chopped fresh parsley

INSTRUCTIONS:

•Season the pork with pepper and mustard and dump into a slow cooker.

•Dump the potatoes, brown sugar and sauerkraut and pour over the beer.

•Cook covered for 6 hours on low.

•Serve garnished with parsley.

Ketogenic Dump Pineapple Chicken Dinner
(Servings: 6)

INGREDIENTS:

- 1/3 cup unsweetened pineapple juice
- 1/4 cup reduced-sodium soy sauce
- 3 tbsp. potato starch, crushed
- 3 tbsp. balsamic vinegar
- 2 tbsp. dry sherry or cider vinegar
- 2 tbsp. tomato paste
- 1 tbsp. honey
- 1 tbsp. minced garlic
- 1 tsp. ground ginger
- 1/2 tsp. cayenne pepper
- 1 medium onion, cut in thin wedges
- 2 medium carrots, peeled and bias-sliced
- 12 small skinless, boneless chicken thighs
- 1 (10 – oz.) package frozen white rice, cooked

INSTRUCTIONS:

•Combine the soy sauce, pineapple juice, balsamic vinegar, potato starch, sherry, honey, tomato paste, ginger, garlic and cayenne in a bowl.

•Place the onions in a slow cooker and dump the carrots and chicken on top.

•Pour the soy sauce mixture spreading it evenly on top.

•Cook covered for 6-7 hours on low.

•Serve the saucy chicken over the rice.

Ketogenic Dump Curried Chicken & Veggies Dinner
(Servings: 8)

INGREDIENTS:

2 cups packaged peeled fresh baby carrots

1 cup regular pearled barley

1 1/2 tsp. minced garlic

3 cups coarsely shredded cabbage

8 bone-in chicken thighs, skin removed (about 3 lbs. total)

2 tbsp. orange marmalade

5 tsp. curry powder

1/2 tsp. salt

1/4 tsp. ground black pepper

3 1/2 cups reduced-sodium chicken broth

1/2 cup unsalted peanuts, coarsely chopped

1/4 cup raisins

1/4 cup sliced green onions

INSTRUCTIONS:

•Whisk the orange marmalade, salt, pepper and curry powder in a bowl.

•Dump the barley, carrots and garlic in a slow cooker and top with the chicken thighs and cabbage.

•Pour the orange marmalade mixture spreading it evenly on top and finally pour the broth.

•Cook covered for 8 hours on low.

•Garnish with raisins, peanuts and green onions.

Ketogenic Dump Jalapeno Beef Dinner
(Servings: 8)

INGREDIENTS:

1 ½ lbs. lean ground beef

1 cup chopped onion

1 clove garlic, minced

1 6 - oz. can vegetable juice

1/2 cup catsup

1/2 cup water

2 tbsp. no-calorie, heat-stable granular sugar substitute

2 tbsp. chopped, canned jalapeno peppers

1 tbsp. prepared mustard

2 tsp. chili powder

1 tsp. Worcestershire sauce

Shredded reduced-fat cheddar cheese

Sweet pepper strips

INSTRUCTIONS:

•Cook the onion, garlic and ground beef in a skillet until browned and transfer to a slow cooker.

•Dump the rest of the ingredients except the cheese and pepper strips in the slow cooker and stir mix.

•Cook covered for 6-8 hours on low.

•Garnish with cheese and pepper strips.

Ketogenic Dump Roasted Veggie & Tomato Soup Dinner
(Servings: 8)

INGREDIENTS:

1 tbsp. olive oil
1 medium onion, chopped
1 stalk celery, sliced
1 medium carrot, chopped
1 tsp. bottled minced garlic
3 14 - oz. cans reduced-sodium chicken broth
2 cups cut-up, peeled, and seeded butternut squash
1 (14 1/2 – oz.) can fire-roasted diced tomatoes
1 (15 – oz.) can white kidney beans, rinsed and drained
1 small zucchini, halved lengthwise and sliced
1 cup small broccoli florets
1 tbsp. snipped fresh oregano
1/4 tsp. salt
1/4 tsp. freshly ground black pepper
Freshly shredded Parmesan cheese

INSTRUCTIONS:

•Heat oil in a Dutch oven and sauté the onion, garlic, celery and carrots in it.
•Mix in the squash, broth and undrained tomatoes and bring to boil.
•Reduce the flame and simmer covered for 20 minutes.
•Dump the rest of the ingredients except the cheese and cook for 5 minutes.
•Garnish with cheese.

Ketogenic Dump Mushroom & Chicken Dinner
(Servings: 6)

INGREDIENTS:

5 cups sliced assorted fresh mushrooms

1 medium onion, chopped

1 medium carrot, chopped

1/4 cup dried tomato pieces

3/4 cup reduced-sodium chicken broth

1/4 cup dry white wine

3 tbsp. quick-cooking tapioca

1 tsp. dried thyme, crushed

1/2 tsp. dried basil, crushed

1/2 tsp. salt

1/4-1/2 tsp. black pepper

12 small chicken thighs, skinned

3 cups low carb pasta

Snipped fresh basil

INSTRUCTIONS:

•Dump all the ingredients in a slow cooker.

•Cook covered for 7-8 hours on low.

•Serve with the pasta and garnish with basil.

Ketogenic Dump Wild Rice & Chicken Soup Dinner
(Servings: 6)

INGREDIENTS:

3 cups water

1 (14 – oz.) can reduced-sodium chicken broth

1 (10 3/4 – oz.) can reduced-fat and reduced-sodium condensed cream of chicken soup

2/3 cup uncooked wild rice, rinsed and drained

1/2 tsp. dried thyme, crushed

1/4 tsp. ground black pepper

3 cups chopped cooked chicken

2 cups shredded fresh spinach

INSTRUCTIONS:

•Dump all the ingredients in a slow cooker except the cooked chicken and spinach.

•Cook covered for 7-8 hours on low.

•Mix in the chicken and spinach.

Ketogenic Dump Pasta with Italian Pork Chops Dinner
(Servings: 6)

INGREDIENTS:

1 medium onion, chopped

6 pork rib chops (with bone), cut 1/2 inch thick

2 tsp. dried Italian seasoning, crushed

4 cloves garlic, minced

1/2 tsp. salt

1/4 tsp. ground black pepper

2 14 1/2 - oz. can no-salt-added diced tomatoes, undrained

2 tbsp. balsamic vinegar

2 medium zucchini, halved lengthwise and cut crosswise into 1-inch pieces

2 tbsp. cornstarch whisked in 2 tbsp. cold water

4 oz. dried orzo, cooked according to package directions

INSTRUCTIONS:

•Layer the onions in a slow cooker and place half the pork chops on top.

•Add half the garlic, salt, pepper and Italian seasoning and then repeat the layering.

•Finally top with the undrained tomatoes, balsamic vinegar and zucchini.

•Cook covered for 8-9 hours on low.

•Transfer the meat and veggies into a plate and add the cornstarch mix to the slow cooker.

•Cook until thickened and then pour over the meat and veggies.

•Serve with the orzo.

Ketogenic Dump Steak Roll Up Dinner
(Servings: 6)

INGREDIENTS:

1 1/2 lbs. beef flank steak, fat trimmed, cut to fit in cooker
1 (16 – oz.) package frozen (yellow, green, and red) peppers and onion stir-fry vegetables
1 (14 1/2 – oz.) can Mexican-style stewed tomatoes
1 small jalapeno pepper, seeded and finely chopped
2 tsp. chili powder
6 (6 - 7 – inches) whole wheat flour tortillas, warmed
Lime wedges

INSTRUCTIONS:

•Dump the meat, frozen veggies, undrained tomatoes, jalapeno pepper and chili powder in a slow cooker.
•Cook covered for 7-8 hours on low.
•Remove and slice the meat against the grain.
•Divide the veggies and meat among the tortillas and roll up.
•Serve with the lime wedges.

Ketogenic Dump Pork Dinner
(Servings: 6)

INGREDIENTS:

1 lb. ground pork
1 large onion, chopped
2 cloves garlic, minced
1 tsp. dried oregano, crushed
1/4 tsp. salt
1/4-1/2 tsp. crushed red pepper
4 cups reduced-sodium chicken broth
12 oz. tiny red new potatoes, each cut into 8 pieces
1 (12 – oz.) can fat-free evaporated milk
2 tbsp. cornstarch
2 cups chopped fresh kale
Crushed red pepper

INSTRUCTIONS:

•Sauté the onions and garlic in a skillet and brown the meat.
•Sprinkle the salt, crushed red pepper and oregano over the meat-onion mixture and cook for a minute.
•Dump the meat mixture along with the broth and potatoes in a slow cooker.
•Cook covered for 6-8 hours on low.
•Whisk the cornstarch with the milk and pour into the slow cooker and stir.
•Cook covered for 30 minutes on high.

Ketogenic Dump Roasted Beef with Mushrooms Dinner
(Servings: 6-8)

INGREDIENTS:

2 lb. Beef Roast
8oz White Mushrooms, sliced
1 Carrot, diced
1 Onion, diced
1 Celery stalk, diced
1 bunch of Parsley, chopped
1 clove Garlic, pressed
2 Tbsp. of Butter
Oil
¾ cup water
Salt and Pepper

INSTRUCTIONS:

•Season the beef with salt and pepper.
•Heat oil and butter in a pressure cooker and throw in the roast.
•Brown the outside of the roast and then dump in the carrots, onion, garlic, parsley, mushrooms, salt, pepper, celery and the water.
•Close the pressure cooker.
•Bring to high pressure on high flame and then reduce the flame once it reaches pressure.
•Cook for 17 minutes.
•Release the pressure naturally and uncover.

Ketogenic Dump Veal Stew Dinner

INGREDIENTS:

2 sprigs fresh rosemary, one finely chopped and one for garnish
1 tbsp. olive oil
1 tbsp. butter
8 oz. shallots
2 carrots, chopped
2 celery stalks, chopped
3 lbs. veal, sliced into 1" cubes and coated with all purpose flour
1 cup white wine
White veal stock
2 tsp. salt - withhold if using salted stock

INSTRUCTIONS:

•Heat oil and butter in the pressure cooker and add the chopped rosemary, shallots, celery and carrots and sauté until the shallots soften.
•Place the veggies aside in the pressure cooker and brown the meat.
•Pour in the wine and deglaze the brown bits.
•Pour in the stock to almost cover the meat and then close the pressure cooker.
•Bring to high pressure on high flame and then reduce the flame once it reaches pressure.
•Cook at high pressure for 15-20 minutes.
•Release the pressure naturally.
•Simmer for another 5 minutes uncovered until it thickens slightly.

Ketogenic Dump Italian Veal Roast Dinner

INGREDIENTS:

2 tbsp. olive oil

1 lb. veal roast

1 onion, roughly sliced

1 carrot, roughly sliced

1 celery stalk, roughly sliced

2 garlic cloves, whole

5 bay leaves

1 rosemary sprig

4 cloves

1 tbsp. salt

1 tsp. freshly ground pepper

1 cup white wine

1 cup water

For the tuna sauce:

3 Anchovies

1- 5½ oz. can of Tuna in Olive Oil, strained

1 cup mayonnaise

2 tbsp. capers, rinsed if salted or drained if in oil

INSTRUCTIONS:

•Brown the meat in oil in the pressure cooker and place aside.

•Sauté the onions, celery and carrots and then throw in the garlic, bay leaves, cloves and rosemary.

•Return the veal roast to the cooker and cover with wine and water seasoning with salt and pepper.

•Close the pressure cooker and bring to pressure on high heat.

•Reduce the heat to maintain pressure and cook for 15-25 minutes.

•Release the pressure naturally, uncover and remove the roast.

•Reserve the stock for later use.

•For the tuna sauce, puree all the sauce ingredients.

•Slice the roast and serve with the tuna sauce.

Ketogenic Dump Pepper Beef Steak Dinner

INGREDIENTS:

2 lbs. round beef steak, cut into serving size pieces
1 tbsp. olive oil
1 can (14.5 oz.) beef broth
1 tbsp. dehydrated onion flakes
1/2 tsp. salt and pepper
1 tsp. garlic powder
1 tsp. onion powder
3/4 cup sliced onion
2 medium green bell peppers, cut into chunks

INSTRUCTIONS:

•Season the steak with pepper and salt and brown it lightly in olive oil.
•Dump the rest of the ingredients in the pressure and close it.
•Bring to full pressure on high heat and then reduce the heat to maintain pressure.
•Cook for 15 minutes and then remove from the flame.
•Release the pressure naturally and uncover.

Ketogenic Dump Anaheim Chile Beef Dinner

INGREDIENTS:

3 lb. beef chuck roast cubes, fat trimmed off
4 tsp. olive oil
1 very large onion, chopped into 1/2 inch pieces
1 tbsp. crushed garlic
2 tbsp. ground Ancho chile peppers
2 tsp. sweet paprika
2 tsp. Mexican oregano
1 tbsp. ground cumin
1/2 cup beef stock
2 cans (10 oz. can) diced tomatoes with green chiles
1 can (4 oz.) diced Anaheim green chiles with juice
salt and fresh ground black pepper to taste
2 tbsp. fresh squeezed lime juice

INSTRUCTIONS:

•Brown the meat in some oil in a pressure cooker and place aside.
•Add the rest of the olive oil and sauté the onions then add the paprika, Ancho chile, garlic, oregano and cumin and cook for a minute after which transfer the spices to the cooker.
•Deglaze the skillet using the beef stock and throw in the tomatoes.
•Bring to high pressure on high heat and then reduce the heat to maintain pressure.
•Cook for 15 minutes and then remove from the flame.
•Release the pressure naturally and uncover.
•Throw in the Anaheim chiles and stir mix.
•Simmer uncovered on low flame until thickened for around 20 minutes.
•Season with salt and pepper and mix in the lime juice.

Ketogenic Dump Sherry Braised Beef Ribs Dinner
(Servings: 4)

INGREDIENTS:

2 tbsp. olive oil, divided

3 lbs. beef short ribs

10 oz. bag pearl onions, ends trimmed and peeled

4 garlic cloves, peeled and sliced

½ cup dry sherry

1 large carrot, top removed, peeled, and cut into large chunks

1 celery stalk, cut into large chunks

1 bay leaf

1 sprig thyme

1 sprig flat leaf parsley

2 cups beef broth

Salt and pepper, to taste

INSTRUCTIONS:

•Season the beef ribs with pepper and salt.

•Heat some olive oil in the pressure cooker over medium flame and brown the ribs in it until golden on both sides. Place aside in a bowl.

•Add another tbsp. of oil and sauté the pearl onions and garlic until lightly browned.

•Pour in sherry and deglaze the bottom.

•Dump the ribs back to the cooker with the celery, carrot, bay leaf, parsley, thyme and beef stock.

•Close the pressure cooker and bring to pressure on high heat.

•Reduce the heat to medium and cook for 45-50 minutes.

•Release the pressure naturally and uncover.

Ketogenic Dump Mustard Short Ribs Dinner
(Servings: 8)

INGREDIENTS:

2 tbsp. seasoned salt

2 tbsp. cassava flour

4lbs. beef short ribs

2 tbsp. coconut oil

1 large onion, chopped

3 cloves garlic, minced or pressed

1 stalk celery, chopped

1 cups diced tomatoes in juice

1 cups beef broth

1 cup dry red wine

2 tbsp. tomato paste

1 tbsp. yellow mustard

1 tbsp. Worcestershire sauce

2 tbsp. honey

1 tsp. cumin

2 bay leaves

1 tsp. seasoned salt

INSTRUCTIONS:

•Combine the cassava flour with 2 tbsp. seasoned salt in a bowl and coat the ribs with it.

•Heat oil in the pressure cooker and brown the ribs in batches and place aside in a plate.

•Sauté the onions and garlic for 5-6 minutes and scrape the brown bits stuck to the bottom.

•Pour in the broth, wine and dump in the tomatoes, mustard, tomato paste, cumin, honey, 1 tsp. seasoned salt, bay leaves and browned ribs and bring to simmer.

•Cover the pressure cooker and bring to pressure.

•Cook for 1 hour under pressure.

•Release the pressure naturally and uncover.
•Place the ribs in a bowl.
•Simmer the sauce on medium flame to thicken it and then dump the ribs back to sauce.

Ketogenic Dump Coffee Roasted Beef Dinner

INGREDIENTS:

1 (3-lb.) beef sirloin tip roast
2 tbsp. vegetable oil
1 medium onion, chopped
2 garlic cloves, minced
2 1/2 cups brewed coffee
2 1/2 cups water, divided
2 beef bouillon cubes
1 tsp. salt
2 tsp. dried basil
1/2 tsp. coarsely ground pepper
1/2 cup all-purpose flour

INSTRUCTIONS:

•Heat oil in the pressure cooker and brown the beef roast along with the onions and garlic.
•Combine the 2 cups water, salt, coffee, bouillon, and basil in a bowl and pour it over the roast.
•Cover the pressure cooker.
•Cook over high heat until the pressure is reached and then reduce the heat.
•Cook for 40 minutes and then remove from the flame.
•Release the pressure using the cold water method and uncover.

Ketogenic Dump BBQ Spare Ribs Dinner
(Servings: 10)

INGREDIENTS:

10 lbs. spare ribs, cut into serving pieces
Salt and pepper
Paprika
3 tsp. vegetable oil
4 onions, sliced
2 cups ketchup
1 cup vinegar
2 tsp. Worcestershire sauce
1 tsp. chili powder
1 tsp. celery seed

INSTRUCTIONS:

•Season the ribs with salt, pepper and paprika.
•Heat oil in the pressure cooker and brown the ribs in it.
•Dump in the onions.
•Combine the rest of the ingredients together in a bowl and pour over the ribs.
•Cover the pressure cooker.
•Cook for 15 minutes at 15 lbs. pressure.
•Release the pressure naturally and uncover.

Ketogenic Dump Rump Steak Italian Style Dinner
(Servings: 15)

INGREDIENTS:

9 lbs. rump steak

3 tsp. cooking oil

3 onions, chopped

2 cups diced celery

3 carrots, chopped

3 bay leaves

1 tsp. salt

2 cups sliced mushrooms

3 (6 oz.) cans tomato paste

2 (10 1/2 oz.) cans beef broth

1 1/2 cups dry red wine

INSTRUCTIONS:

•Heat oil in the pressure cooker and brown the rump steak in it.

•Dump in the veggies and the seasonings.

•Combine the tomato paste with the broth and the wine and pour it over the meat and veggies.

•Cover the pressure cooker.

•Cook for 35 minutes at 15 lbs. pressure.

•Release the pressure naturally and uncover.

Ketogenic Dump Beer Chuck Roast Dinner
(Servings: 4-6)

INGREDIENTS:

1 1/2-2 lbs. chuck roast
3 tbsp. olive oil
2 tbsp. mustard
1 tsp. paprika
1/2 tsp. coarse salt
1/2 tsp. black pepper
12 oz. beer
2 tbsp. flour
2 tbsp. tomato paste
1 cup beef broth
1 large onion
6 carrots

INSTRUCTIONS:

•Heat oil in the pressure cooker, and brown the chuck roast and place aside.
•Add a small amount of beer and deglaze the bottom of the pressure cooker.
•Add the tomato paste and flour and cook for a minute.
•Dump the meat in the cooker along with the rest of the ingredients.
•Cover the pressure cooker and cook for an hour on high pressure.
•Release the pressure naturally and uncover.

Ketogenic Dump Sauerkraut Spare Ribs Dinner
(Servings: 4)

INGREDIENTS:

2 lbs. spare ribs, cut into serving size pieces
1 tbsp. vegetable oil
Salt and pepper
1 quart sauerkraut
1 tbsp. brown sugar
1 ½ cup water

INSTRUCTIONS:

•Heat oil in the pressure cooker, and brown the ribs in it.
•Season with pepper and salt and sprinkle the brown sugar and pour the sauerkraut over the ribs.
•Sprinkle the brown sugar and pour the sauerkraut over the ribs.
•Cover the pressure cooker and place the regulator on the vent pipe.
•Cook for 15 minutes as the pressure regulator rocks slowly.
•Release the pressure using the quick release method and uncover.

Ketogenic Dump Montparnasse Beef Steak Dinner
(Servings: 6)

INGREDIENTS:

2 lbs. beef round steaks, cut into serving pieces

2 tbsp. shortening

2 slices bacon, cooked, crumbled

6 small white onions, peeled

6 new red potatoes, scrubbed

1 can (8 oz. size) mushrooms, with liquid

1/2 cup dry white wine

1 tbsp. parsley, minced

2 tsp. salt

1/2 tsp. black pepper

1 bay leaf

INSTRUCTIONS:

•Melt the shortening in the pressure cooker, and brown the steak in it.

•Dump in the rest of the ingredients.

•Cover the pressure cooker and bring to full pressure over high heat.

•Reduce the heat and cook for 15 minutes.

•Release the pressure naturally and uncover.

•Remove the steak and place in a platter.

•Thicken the gravy and then pour over the steak.

Ketogenic Dump Shredded Beef Steak Dinner
(Servings: 10)

INGREDIENTS:

6 lbs. boneless chuck, cut in 1" cubes
1 tbsp. garlic, minced
1/2 cup red chili sauce
1/2 cup water
1 cup barbecue sauce
2 tbsp. olive oil
1 onion, chopped

INSTRUCTIONS:

•Heat olive oil in a pressure cooker, and sauté garlic in it.
•Brown the meat in the oil and then dump in the rest of the ingredients.
•Cover the pressure cooker and cook for an hour.
•Release the pressure using the quick release method and uncover.
•Place the meat in a bowl and shred it.

Ketogenic Dump Marengo Veal Stew Dinner
(Servings: 8)

INGREDIENTS:

1/4 cup flour
1 tsp. salt
1/2 tsp. thyme
1/4 tsp. black pepper
2 1/2 lbs. veal stew meat, cubed
5 tbsp. oil
3/4 cup onion, chopped
1 clove garlic, chopped
1 cup water
1 cube chicken bouillon
1/2 cup dry white wine
1 cup tomatoes, canned
1 1/2 tsp. parsley
1 bay leaf

INSTRUCTIONS:

•Combine the flour, salt, thyme and pepper and coat the veal in the mixture.
•Heat oil in the cooker and brown the meat in it. Remove and place aside in a bowl.
•Sauté the garlic and onions in the oil and then dump in the rest of the ingredients along with the browned veal stew meat.
•Close the pressure cooker and after the control jiggles cook for 15 minutes.
•Release the pressure under cold water.
•Mix the remaining flour with ½ cup water and add to the liquid in the pressure cooker.
•Place over medium flame until thickened, stirring continuously.

Ketogenic Dump Chicken & Potato Soup Dinner
(Servings: 6)

INGREDIENTS:

1 1/2 lbs. chicken thighs (4 thighs)

1 tbsp. olive oil

1 lb. potato, cut into large dice

3/4 lb. yucca root cut into large dice

1 ear of corn, cut into 1 inch rounds

4 cups chicken stock

1 medium onion, chopped

3 garlic cloves, minced

1 cup water

1/4 cup heavy cream

1 tbsp. capers

1 tsp. cayenne pepper

Salt & freshly ground black pepper

Cilantro, for garnish

INSTRUCTIONS:

•Heat oil in a pressure cooker, and brown the chicken pieces seasoned with salt and pepper.

•Dump in the potatoes, yucca, corn, salt, pepper, cayenne and the chicken stock.

•Sauté the onions and garlic in a skillet until soft and pour a cup of water to loosen the bits stuck to the skillet. Transfer to the pressure cooker.

•Cover the cooker and over medium flame for 30 minutes.

•Add the cilantro, capers and cream and stir mix.

Ketogenic Dump Chicken & Corn Chowder Dinner
(Servings: 6-8)

INGREDIENTS:

1/4 lb. bacon, cut into 1-inch pieces
1/4 cup olive oil
1 large onion, diced
3 garlic cloves, slivered
2 chicken breasts (with or without bone)
16 oz. crushed tomatoes
1/4 cup salsa
1 bell pepper, coarsely chopped (green, red, yellow or orange)
2 cups chicken broth
1 tsp. salt
1/2 tsp. crushed red pepper flakes
1/8 tsp. hot pepper sauce (such as Tabasco)
16 oz. whole kernel corn
4 -6 oz. carrots
1/2 cup chopped cilantro
1 tbsp. sherry wine
3 tbsp. all-purpose flour
3 tbsp. butter, softened

INSTRUCTIONS:

•Sauté the bacon until crisp in a pressure cooker.
•Sauté the onions, garlic and chicken in oil.
•Dump in the tomatoes, peppers, salsa, carrots, salt, chicken broth, hot pepper sauce and red pepper flakes.
•Close the pressure cooker and heat on high until full pressure is reached.
•Reduce the flame and cook for 6 minutes.
•Release the pressure and remove the chicken.
•Chop the chicken into bite size pieces and put back into the soup.

•Add the cilantro, corn and sherry to the soup and bring to simmer for 2 minutes.
•Stir mix the butter and flour into a paste and add a tbsp. at a time to the soup, until it gets creamy.
•Cook for a minute more.

Ketogenic Dump Sweet & Sour Chinese Chicken Dinner
(Servings: 4-6)

INGREDIENTS:

3 lbs. roasting chicken, cut up
1 tbsp. vegetable oil
1/2 cup sliced celery
1 bell pepper, cut into chunks
1 (20 oz.) can pineapple chunks, drained and juice reserved
1 cup reserved pineapple juice
1/4 cup brown sugar
1/2 cup vinegar
2 tbsp. soy sauce
1 tbsp. ketchup
1/2 tsp. Worcestershire sauce
1/4 tsp. ground ginger
2 tbsp. cornstarch
2 tbsp. cold water

INSTRUCTIONS:

•Brown the chicken pieces in batches in oil heated in a pressure cooker.
•Dump all the chicken in the pressure cooker with the green pepper and celery.
•Mix the brown sugar, pineapple juice, vinegar, soy sauce, Worcestershire sauce, ginger and ketchup and add it to the chicken.
•Close the pressure cooker.
•Cook at 15 lbs. pressure for 8 minutes, with the regulator rocking.
•Release the pressure using the cold water method.
•Place the chicken and the veggies onto a platter.
•Combine the cornstarch with the water and pour it into the liquid in the pressure cooker.
•Cook until it thickens and then transfer over the chicken.

Ketogenic Dump Garlic & Butter Chicken Dinner
(Servings: 4)

INGREDIENTS:

6 -8 pieces meaty chicken
2 tbsp. butter
1 sliced onion
Minced garlic
1 cup water
1/2 cup soy sauce
1/2 tsp. salt
1/8 tsp. pepper
1/2 tsp. nutmeg

INSTRUCTIONS:

•Melt the butter in a pressure cooker and brown the chicken pieces along with the minced garlic and onion.
•Dump all the remaining ingredients in the pressure cooker and heat on high, till the pressure cooker starts to rock.
•Reduce the heat to medium and cook for 15 minutes.

Ketogenic Dump Gingerroot Chicken Drumsticks Dinner
(Servings: 3)

INGREDIENTS:

¼ cup soy sauce
1 tbsp. olive oil
1 tbsp. gingerroot, finely chopped
2 carrots, chopped
2 scallions, trimmed and sliced
8 chicken drumsticks

INSTRUCTIONS:

•Heat oil in a pressure cooker and brown the chicken drumsticks in it until golden brown.
•Throw in the gingerroot and soy sauce.
•Cover the pressure cooker and cook for 30 minutes.
•Prior to the last 5 minutes of cooking dump the scallions and the carrots.

Ketogenic Dump Sausage & Chicken Stew Dinner
(Servings: 4-6)

INGREDIENTS:

2 -3 lbs. whole chicken breasts, with bone cut into smaller pieces
2 tbsp. butter
1 tbsp. olive oil
2 celery ribs, chopped
1 large onion, chopped
4 garlic cloves, minced
4 carrots, sliced
6 medium potatoes cut into quarters
1 cup white pearl onion
3 cups baby portabella mushrooms, thickly sliced
6 cups chicken broth
14 oz. of hillshire lite smoked sausage, sliced thickly
2 tsp. Cajun seasoning
1 pinch thyme
Salt and pepper

INSTRUCTIONS:

•Heat olive oil and butter in a pressure cooker and sauté the garlic and onions in it.
•Throw in the chicken and mix it up and brown the chicken, turning it often.
•Dump in the rest of the ingredients and ensure that the pressure cooker is no more than two-thirds full, with the broth just covering the ingredients.
•Bring to pressure and cook for 45 minutes.
•Remove the pressure cooker from the heat.
•Release the pressure using the natural release method.

Book 3: Ketogenic Diet Freezer Meals

Freezer Meal Tips

To effectively freeze your meals, there are some easy guidelines you need to follow. Following the guidelines below will help your freezer meals stay fresh and delicious and most importantly prevent them from being ruined.

•Your freezer temp should be below 0 degrees Fahrenheit. This can easily be checked by using a thermometer.

•Make sure you cover and/or wrap the foods very well and to keep track of what is in your freezer.

•If you plan on thawing or defrosting your meals in the microwave, make sure to use microwave safe plastic wrap.

•Its best to freeze your meals in smaller portions so the food cools quicker and defrosts faster for best quality.

•You can freeze ingredients for a casserole in individual bags then put the smaller bags into one large bag. Label well, including thawing and baking instructions, then freeze.

•Remember that freezing will not enhance foods, it will just keep them at their original freshness and quality. Freeze only top quality foods.

FOOD	STORAGE TIME	SPECIAL TIPS
BREADS, MUFFINS	Up to 1 month	Cool completely before freezing. Do not frost. To thaw, loosen wrap and let sit at room temp 2-3 hours. To heat, wrap in foil, reheat 350 degrees 15-20 minutes. Heat frozen waffles without thawing first.
SANDWICHES	Up to 2 weeks	Don't make sandwiches with jelly, mayonnaise, cooked egg whites or raw veggies (especially lettuce). Choose peanut butter, cream cheese, meats, shredded cheeses, grilled and cooked veggies. Spread bread with a very thin layer of butter before layering.
VEGETABLES	Up to 6 months	Blanch before freezing. Remove as much air as possible from package before freezing. Vegetables with lots of water like salad greens and tomatoes do not freeze well. Do not freeze deep fried vegetables.
FRUITS	Up to 6 months	Up to 1 year Freeze loose small fruits in single layer on cookie sheet until firm; then package in airtight freezer bag or container and freeze. Thaw in refrigerator.
SAUCES	Up to 3 months	Most sauces will separate after being frozen. If mixed with other ingredients, freezing quality will increase. Sauces with cornstarch and cheese lose quality fastest. Leave some head space for expansion when freezing in plastic containers.
CASSEROLES	Up to 3 months	Cornstarch sauces can be frozen when mixed with other ingredients in a casserole. Slightly undercook casseroles, as they will finish cooking during reheating.
SOUPS	Up to 6 months	Cool completely, skim off fat. Place in rigid plastic containers, leaving 1/2" head space for expansion.
MEATS	Fresh: 1 year Cured: 1 month	Do NOT refreeze thawed meats. If you thaw frozen meat, cook it in some form, then it can be refrozen. Cured meats should be frozen for just one month. Do NOT freeze stuffed chicken or turkey. Make sure to reform ground beef into thin patties before freezing for quick thawing.
FISH	Up to 3 months	Wrap tightly in heavy duty freezer wrap or plastic bags. Thaw overnight in refrigerator before cooking.
COOKED PASTAS	Up to 2 months	Cooked pastas lose quality when frozen. Undercook and freeze in a sauce for best results. Thaw overnight in refrigerator before reheating.

Ketogenic Freezer Coconut Peanut Curry Soup

INGREDIENTS:

¾ cup smooth peanut butter

1 can fire-roasted diced tomatoes

1 can unsweetened light coconut milk

2 cup low-sodium chicken broth

2 cups shredded rotisserie chicken

2 Tbsp. madras curry paste

INSTRUCTIONS:

•In a saucepan, whisk curry paste and broth.

•Heat the mixture over medium heat to boil.

•Whisk in peanut butter and coconut milk, and then simmer for two to three minutes.

•Add in the tomatoes and chicken, and continue cooking until heated well.

•To taste, season with kosher salt.

FREEZING INSTRUCTIONS:

•Allow the soup to cool down at room temperature.

•Place it in a plastic food storage container and don't forget to date and label.

•You can keep it in the freezer for two to three months.

SERVING INSTRUCTIONS:

•Remove from the freezer and let it thaw in the fridge overnight.

•Transfer it in a saucepan and heat. If you want, you can sprinkle chopped roasted peanuts and •garnish with lime wedges.

NUTRITIONAL VALUES:

Calories   527

Carbs   10g

Fats   37g

Protein   35g

Ketogenic Freezer Cheesy Bouillon Reuben Soup

INGREDIENTS:

1 cup sauerkraut, well drained

1(12 oz.) package Swiss cheese, shredded

½ cup chopped onion

½ lb. cooked and shredded corned beef

¼ cup chopped celery

¼ cup unsifted flour

3 cup half-and-half

3 cup water

3 tbsp. butter or 3 tbsp. margarine

4 tsp. beef bouillon or 4 beef bouillon cubes

6 -8 slices pumpernickel bread or 6 -8 slices rye bread toasted and quartered

INSTRUCTIONS:

•In a big saucepan, sauté celery and onion in butter until tender.

•Add in the flour mix until smooth.

•Slowly add in the bouillon and water and let it boil.

•Lower the heat and simmer without covering for 5 mins.

•Add sauerkraut, 1 cup cheese, corned beef, and half and half.

•Cook for thirty minutes, until it thickens, with frequent stirring.

•Pour into 8 oven proof bowls.

•Place toasted bread and cheese on top.

•Broil until the cheese melts.

FREEZING INSTRUCTIONS:

•Before pouring it in a plastic food storage container, let the soup cool down at room temperature.

•Don't forget to label and date.

•Store in the freezer the soup will last for two to three months.

SERVING INSTRUCTIONS:

•Remove from freezer and allow it to thaw in the fridge overnight.
•Pour it in the saucepan and set over medium heat.
•If you want, you can add chopped roasted peanuts on top and garnish it with lime wedges.

NUTRITIONAL VALUE:

Calories	474
Carbs	22.8g
Fats	32.8g
Protein	22.2g

Ketogenic Freezer Broccoli Chicken Cheese Soup

INGREDIENTS:

¼ cup Butter
¼ cup Flour, All-Purpose
¼ tsp. Nutmeg
½ cup dice Onion
½ tsp. Salt
1 ½ cup Broccoli Cuts, Frozen
1 cup dice Carrot
1 tsp. Black Pepper
2 cup Chicken Broth/Stock
2 cup Half and Half
2 cup shredded Cheddar Cheese

INSTRUCTIONS:

•Over medium heat, place and melt in a stock pan the butter and then add the flour. Whisk together for three to four minutes.
•Gradually add the chicken stock, and half and half, continue whisking together.
•Continue cooking over medium heat until it starts to simmer.
•Adjust the heat to low once it starts to simmer.
•Add the broccoli, onion and carrots. Continue cooking for another ten minutes or until the vegetables are cooked.
•Add cheese, salt and pepper. Once the cheese melts, don't forget to stir mix well.
•Add the nutmeg as soon as the cheese has melted and remove it from heat. The soup will have vegetable chunks.

FREEZING INSTRUCTIONS:

•Allow it to cool down completely. Divide on the desired number of freezer bags.
•Label, date and freeze.

SERVING INSTRUCTIONS:

•Reheat the soup in a microwave for one to two minutes or until thoroughly warmed.

NUTRITIONAL VALUE:

Calories	326
Carbs	3g
Fats	32g
Protein	5g

Ketogenic Freezer Creamy Cauliflower, Bacon and Chicken Soup

INGREDIENTS:

¼ cup heavy cream
1 head of cauliflower
1 medium onion
1 oz. Parmesan cheese
1 Tbsp. minced garlic
1 tsp. ground thyme
12 oz. Cheddar cheese
2 Tbsp. of olive oil
3 cup chicken broth
4 slices of bacon

INSTRUCTIONS:

•Prepare the cauliflower, cut it into small florets and arrange them in a baking sheet with oil.
•Season it with pepper and salt and bake at 375 degrees Fahrenheit for thirty minutes or until it becomes golden brown.
•As the cauliflower is baking, microwave or pan-fry the bacon until it becomes crispy.
•Keep the bacon drippings and sauté the chopped onion in the oil.
•Sprinkle on top the dried thyme and cook until all the flavors blended together, for one minute.
•Add in the broth and then add the roasted cauliflower in the saucepan.
•Boil at low heat for about fifteen minutes.
•Place the ingredients in a blender or food processor, or you can use an immersion stick blender.
•As soon as you achieve the desired consistency, slowly add the cheese until it melts completely followed by the bacon and the heavy cream.

FREEZING INSTRUCTIONS:

•Allow the soup to cool down at room temperature.

•Pour in plastic storage container and label and date.

•Store in the freezer, the soup may last up to two to three months.

SERVING INSTRUCTIONS:

•Take it out from the freezer and let it thaw in the fridge overnight.

•Pour in a saucepan and heat.

NUTRITIONAL VALUE:

Calories 337
Carbs   11g
Fats   25g
Protein 18g

Ketogenic Freezer Creamy Chicken

INGREDIENTS:

2 (4 oz. each) boneless, skinless chicken breasts
2 oz. jalapeno slices
4 oz. cheddar cheese
4 slices of bacon
Half pinch of pepper to taste
Pinch of salt

INSTRUCTIONS:

•Season the chicken breasts with pepper and salt.
•Sprinkle 2 oz. of cheese on each chicken breasts.
•To make it spicy add jalapeno slices.
•Drape over the chicken breasts the bacon.

FREEZING INSTRUCTIONS:

•In a foil-lined pan, place the chicken breasts and use foil to cover it.

•Write the name of the dish and date in the foil and also the cooking INSTRUCTIONS.
•Store in the freezer and it will last up to six months.

SERVING INSTRUCTIONS:

•Take it out from the freezer and allow it to thaw in the fridge overnight.
•Heat the oven at 350 degrees Fahrenheit for thirty to forty five minutes or until cooked.
•Broil for about 2 mins. for crisper bacon.

NUTRITIONAL VALUE:

Calories	296
Carbs	1 g
Fats	16.5 g
Protein	35 g

Ketogenic Freezer Easy Chicken

INGREDIENTS:

32 oz. skinless, boneless chicken breasts
Canola oil spray
Pepper to taste
Salt to taste

INSTRUCTIONS:

•Prepare the chicken, slice it into pieces around one inch thick.
•In a baking dish spray canola oil and arrange the chicken in the pan.
•Season chicken breasts with salt and pepper.
•Bake at 350 degrees Fahrenheit for about thirty minutes.

FREEZING INSTRUCTIONS:

•Place in a container and with the use of plastic wrap cover and let it cool completely in the fridge.
•To store the chicken, use gallon size zip top bags and lay it flat in the freezer.
•Once the chicken is frozen, shake the bag to break the chicken up and remove any excess air and then reseal the bag.

SERVING INSTRUCTIONS:

Take it out from the freezer and allow it to thaw in the fridge before heating it.

NUTRITIONAL VALUE:

Calories   125
Carbs   0g
Fats   1.5g
Protein   26g

Ketogenic Freezer Avocado Baked Chicken

INGREDIENTS:

1 chopped medium onion
1 sliced medium pepper
1 Tbsp. Frank's Red Hot Sauce
4 small pitted sliced avocados
8 cooked boneless chicken thighs
8 oz. cheddar cheese
8 oz. regular sour cream
To taste, pepper and salt

INSTRUCTIONS:

•Pre-heat your oven at 350 degrees Fahrenheit.
•Place the chicken thighs in the oven and bake for one hour or until the juices run clear.
•Prepare the avocados. First cut the avocado lengthwise. Remove the pit then whack it using the knife. Slowly twist the knife to remove the pit from the avocado. Scoop out the avocado flesh using a spoon.
•Put some oil in the baking dish and then add the avocado slices in the bottom.
•Save some for later.
•Over medium heat, fry the onions and pepper until caramelized.
•Use fork to shred the chicken.
•Add the rest of the ingredients to the shredded chicken, together with the extra avocado and place it over the bottom layer of avocado slices.
•Bake for twenty minutes.

FREEZING INSTRUCTIONS:

•Allow the casserole to cool down, cover the dish with cling wrap then foil.

•Before storing in the freezer, label and date the dish. It can last up to six months.

SERVING INSTRUCTIONS:

•Take the dish out of the freezer and allow it to thaw in the fridge.
•Heat the dish thoroughly in the oven.

NUTRITIONAL VALUE:

Calories	549
Carbs	13g
Fats	40g
Protein	39g

Ketogenic Freezer Creamy Mushroom Soup

INGREDIENTS:

1 can cream of mushroom soup
1 can diet Sprite
1 pack onion soup mix
2 lbs. beef chuck arm roast, one-eight inches fat, slice into 1 ¾ inch
Onions or cauliflower

INSTRUCTIONS:

•Add the meat in the casserole dish.
•Combine onion soup mix and cream of mushroom soup in separate bowl.
•Add the mixture in the meat.
•Add one can of diet Sprite.

FREEZING INSTRUCTIONS:

•Cover the dish tightly and store in the freezer.

SERVING INSTRUCTIONS:

•Remove the dish from the freezer and allow it to thaw inside the fridge overnight.
•Put all the contents in the crockpot.
•Cook on high for about 4 hours or on low for 8-10 hours.
•Turn off the heat. Let it stand for around 30 mins. before serving to allow the juices set into the meat.

NUTRITIONAL VALUE:

Calories   400
Carbs   6g
Fats   25g
Protein   35g

Ketogenic Freezer Thai Broccoli Chicken

INGREDIENTS:

1 (14 oz.) can coconut milk
1 cup chicken broth or 1 cup chicken stock
1 can bamboo shoot, drained
1 lb. chicken breast, cut into 1/2 " strips
1 tbsp. green curry paste or red curry paste
1/4 cup fresh basil
2 tbsps. brown sugar
3 -4 cup fresh broccoli florets
3 tbsps. fish sauce

INSTRUCTIONS:

Combine coconut milk and curry paste in a medium saucepan and heat.
Before it starts to boil, reduce the heat and then simmer for five minutes.
Add the rest of the ingredients and then simmer for another ten to fifteen minutes.
You can serve it immediately or store in the freezer.

FREEZING INSTRUCTIONS:

•Allow the soup to cool down at room temperature.
•Pour in plastic storage container and label and date.
•Store in the freezer, the soup may last up to two to three months.

SERVING INSTRUCTIONS:

•Take it out from the freezer and allow it to thaw in the fridge before heating it.
•Serve over freshly cooked rice.

Ketogenic Freezer Thai Green Curry Chicken

INGREDIENTS:

1 tbsp. peanut or vegetable oil

2 to 4 oz. Thai green curry paste

2 13.5-oz. cans coconut milk

1 1/2 lbs. skinless, boneless chicken thighs or breast, cut into one inch pieces

8 oz. cuttlefish balls, thawed, optional

1 lb. zucchini, cut into thick half-moons

To taste add Fish sauce, sugar, soy sauce

INSTRUCTIONS:

•In a heavy pot or 4-quart Dutch oven, heat the oil over medium-high heat. Add the curry paste over heated oil. Be careful, as it will sputter.

•Pan-fry the past for two minutes with frequent stirring.

•Make sure that the vent or fan is turned on since it will be quite pungent.

•Scoop out the solid part in the cans of coconut milk. Set aside the watery part.

•Fry these solids together with the curry paste for about two minutes, until the oil begins to separate out, producing beads over the curry paste.

•Stir in the chicken pieces and stir to combine.

•Add the watery part of the coconut milk together with the cuttlefish balls.

•Adjust the heat to medium-low and simmer for another twenty minutes, or until the fish balls are warm and the chicken is cooked.

•Once the chicken is cooked, add the zucchini and then continue to simmer until it becomes soft and tender.

•Taste and season with sugar, soy sauce, and fish sauce.

•You can serve it right away or store in the freezer.

FREEZING INSTRUCTIONS:

•Allow it to cool down completely. Divide on the desired number of freezer bags.
•Label, date and freeze.

SERVING INSTRUCTIONS:

•Take it out from the freezer and thaw in the fridge overnight.
•Heat in the saucepan.
•Serve with rice noodles or rice.

NUTRITIONAL VALUE:

Calories   372
Carbs   10.6 g
Fat   26.3 g
Protein   27.9 g

Ketogenic Freezer Healthy Soup

INGREDIENTS:

¼ cup ghee or coconut oil

1 cup cream *or* 240ml coconut milk + 6 Tbsp. for garnish

1 crumbled bay leaf

1 medium head cauliflower, cut into small florets

1 medium white onion

1 tsp. salt or to taste

2 cloves garlic

4 cup vegetable stock *or* chicken stock

5.3 oz. watercress

7.1 oz. fresh spinach

Fresh herbs such as chives or parsley for garnish (optional)

Freshly ground black pepper

INSTRUCTIONS:

•Finely dice the garlic and onion and cook until brown over a medium-high heat in Dutch oven or soup pot greased with ghee.

•Wash the watercress and spinach and put aside.

•Place the cauliflower in the pot with onion. Add the bay leaf and cook for five minutes with frequent stirring.

•Add the watercress and spinach and cook for about two to three minutes or until wilted.

•Add the vegetable stock and boil. Cook until the cauliflower becomes crisp-tender and add the coconut milk.

•Season with pepper and salt. Remove from heat and use a hand blender to make the soup smooth and creamy.

FREEZING INSTRUCTIONS:

•Allow the soup to cool down at room temperature.

•Place it in a plastic food storage container and don't forget to date and label.

SERVING INSTRUCTIONS:

•Take it out from the freezer and thaw in the fridge overnight.
•Heat in the saucepan.
•Drizzle some cream on top. Enjoy!

NUTRITIONAL VALUE:

Calories   347
Carbs   6.8g
Fats   37.6g
Protein   4.9g

Ketogenic Freezer Tex Mex Soup

INGREDIENTS:

¼ cup ghee
¼ cup unsweetened tomato puree
1 L. bone broth *or* water
1 large tin tomatoes, unsweetened
1 medium red pepper
1 medium white onion
1 lb. ground beef
1 tsp. salt to taste
2 cup green beans
2 cloves garlic
2 medium fresh tomatoes
2 small green chilies
7 oz. sausage
dash Tabasco *or* to taste
freshly ground black pepper
Optional: parsley or fresh cilantro

INSTRUCTIONS:

•Slice the red and green peppers in halve. Peel and dice the garlic and onion.
•Spread ghee in a Dutch oven or large soup pot. Add the diced garlic and onion on hot ghee and cook over med-high heat for few minutes with frequent stirring, until it becomes lightly browned.
•Add the sliced green chili peppers and sliced red pepper.
•Continue cooking for about five minutes and stir to avoid burning.
•Slice the sausage and chop the tomatoes.
•Add the ground beef, sausage into the pot and cook until browned on all sides.
•Add the tinned tomatoes, Tabasco, chopped tomatoes and tomato puree.

•Add in the water and season with pepper and salt. Wash and slice the green beans. Continue cooking the soup until you see the bubbles and add the green beans.
•Cook until the green beans become crisp and tender or for about 10 mins.
•Turn off the heat. Serve hot with keto buns.

FREEZING INSTRUCTIONS:

•Allow the soup to cool down at room temperature.
•Place it in a plastic food storage container and don't forget to date and label.

SERVING INSTRUCTIONS:

•Take it out from the freezer and thaw in the fridge overnight.
•Heat in the saucepan.

NUTRITIONAL VALUE:

Calories   685.7
Carbs   6.4g
Fats   29.2 g
Protein   18.4g

Ketogenic Freezer Fruits & Veggies Soup

INGREDIENTS:

1 cup extra virgin olive oil
1 large cucumber
1 large or 2 small green peppers
1 large or 2 small red peppers
1 small red onion
1 tsp. salt or to taste
2 cloves garlic
2 medium avocados
2 medium spring onions
2 Tbsp. fresh lemon juice
2 Tbsp. apple cider or wine vinegar
2-4 Tbsp. each freshly chopped basil and parsley
4-5 medium tomatoes
7 oz. soft goat cheese
Freshly ground black pepper

INSTRUCTIONS:

•Roast the peppers first. Preheat the oven to 400 degrees Fahrenheit. Slice the peppers into two and remove the seeds. On a lined baking sheet place the peppers cut side down and place in the oven. Bake the peppers until the skin blisters and turns black or for about 20 mins.
•Meanwhile, peel and cut the red onion and add in the pot if you are using a hand blender or in the blender.
•Slice the tomatoes into 4. Cut the avocados into two, deseed. Add in the pot with the onion.
•Once the peppers are done, take it out from the oven and allow them to cool down. Once cooled, remove the skins and discard. Add the pepper into the pot.
•Add the peeled garlic, vinegar, fresh herbs, olive oil, lemon juice and salt.

•With the use of a hand blender, pulse the mixture until smooth. Use olive oil to garnish. If you have a blender, process all the ingredients until smooth and creamy.
•Slice the spring onions and dice the cucumber. Add the cucumber and onions to the processed soup and mix until well combined. Add pepper and salt to season.

FREEZING INSTRUCTIONS:

•Allow the soup to cool down at room temperature.
•Place it in a plastic food storage container and don't forget to date and label.

SERVING INSTRUCTIONS:

•Take it out from the freezer and thaw in the fridge overnight.
•Heat in the saucepan.
•Top with fresh herbs, crumbled feta cheese and a drizzle of olive oil.

NUTRITIONAL VALUE:

Calories   186
Carbs   8.5 g
Fats   50.8g
Protein   7.5g

Ketogenic Freezer Chili

INGREDIENTS:

¼ cup tomato puree, unsweetened
¼ tsp. cayenne pepper
¼ tsp. black pepper
1 ¼ cup chicken stock, bone broth, or vegetable stock
1 ¼ tsp. ground cumin
1 cup shredded cheddar cheese
1 medium white onion
1 Tbsp. chili powder
1 tsp. dried oregano
1 tsp. salt or more to taste
1 tsp. paprika (regular or smoked)
1.1 lb. minced beef
1-2 bay leaves
2 large sirloin / rump steaks
2 Tbsp. cocoa powder, unsweetened
2 Tbsps. coconut aminos
2 Tbsps. fish sauce
3 Tbsp. ghee or lard
4 cloves garlic

INSTRUCTIONS:

•Over a med-high heat, place a pan and grease with ghee. Add the peel and dice garlic and onion until it fragrant and lightly browned. Mix to avoid burning.
•Cut the sirloin into 1 inch dice and add in the pan along with the minced beef. Continue cooking over med-high heat until it becomes brown from all sides.

149

•Combine all the dry spices- paprika, black pepper, cumin, dried oregano, chili powder and cocoa powder. Add the dry spices, bay leaves and tomato puree to the pan with the beef. Add salt to season and mix well.

•Add the fish sauce, bone broth and coconut aminos. Adjust the heat to medium, cover and simmer for around 45 mins. or until the meat becomes tender.

•Cut the green pepper into two and remove the seeds. Add the green pepper into the pan. Cover and then simmer for another ten minutes. Remove from heat and put aside. Take the bay leaves out.

FREEZING INSTRUCTIONS:

•Allow the dish to cool down at room temperature.

•Place it in a plastic food storage container and don't forget to date and label.

SERVING INSTRUCTIONS:

•Take it out from the freezer and thaw in the fridge overnight. Heat in the saucepan.

•Sprinkle shredded cheese on top.

NUTRITIONAL VALUE:

Calories   492
Carbs   6.1g
Fats   41.9g
Protein   39.1g

Ketogenic Freezer Chicken BBQ Pizza Soup

INGREDIENTS:

¼ ghee or lard
½ tsp. freshly ground black pepper
¾ cup Spicy Chocolate BBQ Sauce
1 ½ cup shredded mozzarella cheese
1 large chicken or 4-6 chicken legs
1 large tin tomatoes, unsweetened
1 medium red onion
1 tsp. salt
2-3 cup water
4 cup green beans
4 cloves garlic
Fresh cilantro *or* basil for garnish

INSTRUCTIONS:

•Preparing the chicken.
•Remove the skin of the chicken and put it in a pot filled with water.
•Add salt and cover. Boil. Lower the heat to med-low once it starts to boil and cook for 60-75 mins. You will know when the chicken is cooked, if the meat comes off easily and pale.
•Place the chicken in the bowl and allow it to cool down slightly.
•Making the soup using the chicken stock.
•In making the soup, you will need two liters of the chicken stock. Put aside the remaining chicken stock for other recipes. You can store it in the fridge for up to five days or if you want longer you can freeze it.
•With a fork, shred the chicken meat off the bones and put aside. Dice the garlic and red onion. •In a large pot with ghee, add the garlic and onion and cook over a medium heat until it becomes fragrant and lightly browned. Add in the chicken stock and let it boil over a high heat.

•Keep the chicken bones; you might need it in the future. You can make a Keto bone broth using the chicken bones.
•For the meantime, wash and cut off the stalks of the green beans, cut them into smaller pieces and then add in the pot along with the tinned tomatoes. Allow it to boil until the green beans are tender for around ten to fifteen minutes.
•Add shredded chicken and BBQ sauce and remove it from heat. Add additional salt if needed and add freshly ground black pepper.
•Grate the pizza type mozzarella cheese.

FREEZING INSTRUCTIONS:

•Allow the dish to cool down at room temperature.
•Place it in a plastic food storage container and don't forget to date and label.
•Store in the freezer for up to six months.

SERVING INSTRUCTIONS:

•Take it out from the freezer and thaw in the fridge overnight. Heat in the saucepan.
•Sprinkle shredded mozzarella cheese on top. Garnish with cilantro

NUTRITIONAL VALUE:

Calories   246.5
Carbs   7.1g
Fats   32.5g
Protein   30.8g

Ketogenic Freezer Baked Avocado Chicken

INGREDIENTS:

1 medium finely diced or chopped onion
1 medium pepper, sliced
1 Tbsp. Frank's Red Hot Sauce
4 small sliced pitted avocados
8 cooked, boneless chicken thighs
8 oz. cheddar cheese
8 oz. regular sour cream
Pepper and salt, to taste

INSTRUCTIONS:

•Pre-heat your oven to 350 degrees Fahrenheit.
•Bake chicken until the juices run clear or for one hour.
•Prepare the avocados. Cut the avocado lengthwise with a sharp knife. Remove the pit and scoop out the avocado flesh with a spoon.
•Oil the baking dish and add the slices of avocado to the bottom. Save some for later.
•Fry the onions and pre-sliced pepper over med-high heat until caramelized.
•Shred the chicken with a fork.
•Add the rest of the ingredients to the chicken, as well as the extra avocado and place over the bottom layer of the avocado slices.
•Bake for twenty minutes.

FREEZING INSTRUCTIONS:

•As soon as the casserole is cooled, use cling wrap then foil to cover it tightly.
•Don't forget to label and date and store in the freezer for six months.

SERVING INSTRUCTIONS:

•Take it out from the freezer and allow it to thaw overnight in the fridge then heat in the oven.

NUTRITIONAL VALUE:

Calories   549
Carbs   13g
Fats   40g
Protein   39g

Ketogenic Freezer Cheesy Chicken Casserole

INGREDIENTS:

1 cup sour cream
16 oz. green salsa
4 oz. diced green chiles
4 stalks diced green onions
4 tsp. taco seasoning mix
8 chicken breasts boneless, skinless
8 oz. Monterey jack cheese

INSTRUCTIONS:

•Cut the chicken breasts into chunks.
•Preheat your oven at 350 degrees Fahrenheit and cook the chicken breast chunks for about thirty minutes.
•In a bowl pour cooked chicken and taco seasoning and toss.
•Place taco chicken in a casserole dish.
•Combine chilies, salsa and sour cream together and pour on top of the chicken.

FREEZING INSTRUCTIONS:

•Allow the casserole to cool down completely, and then cover it with cling wrap and then with foil wrap.
•Store in the freezer.

SERVING INSTRUCTIONS:

•Allow the casserole to thaw in the ref overnight.
•Set your oven at 350 degrees Fahrenheit.
•Sprinkle the jack cheese while the chicken is cooking.
•As soon as the chicken is cooked, remove and cover in cheese and continue cooking for another five minutes.
•Allow it to cool down and slice into pieces, transfer in plastic food storage containers and sprinkle green onions on top.

NUTRITIONAL VALUE:

Calories   351
Carbs   7g
Fats   17g
Protein   34g

Ketogenic Freezer Pork with Mushrooms and Sour Cream

INGREDIENTS:

2/3 cup light sour cream
1 lb. pork loin, remove the fat and cut into cubes 1" square
1/2 cup chicken stock
1 Tbsp. + 1 Tbsp. sweet paprika
salt and fresh ground black pepper (to season the pork)
1 (14.5 oz. can) petite dice tomatoes plus juice
2-3 Tbsp. olive oil
1 finely chopped onion
8-12 oz. crimini or white mushrooms
1/2 tsp. dried thyme
1 Tbsp. finely minced garlic
1/2 tsp. dried caraway seeds, crushed or ground

INSTRUCTIONS:

•Remove all visible fat from pork loin or pork chops roast, then cut into one inch cube square. •Place the meat in a bowl and add sweet paprika and black pepper. Toss.

•In a heavy frying pan with cover, heat 1 Tbsp. olive oil. Brown the meat over med-high heat, change sides several times so all parts are cooked well for around five to six minutes.

•Transfer the meat in another dish and add another Tbsp. of olive oil in the pan, add the mushrooms and cook until all the liquid has evaporated and nicely browned for around five minutes or more. Transfer mushrooms on the same dish with the pork.

•Add more olive oil if needed, stir fry onion and cook until it starts to brown, for around three to five minutes.

•Add garlic, dried thyme, 1 Tbsp. paprika and crushed or ground caraway seeds and cook for around one to two minutes. Add diced tomatoes with juice and chicken stock, simmer and cook for ten minutes, or until it is slightly thickened and the flavors are well-mixed.

•After ten minutes add the mushrooms and browned meat back in the pan, cover and then simmer for another ten minutes, or until the meat is cooked through. Turn off the heat, add in sour cream and serve.

FREEZING INSTRUCTIONS:

•Allow the soup to cool down. To speed up the cooling process, you can stir the soup to release the heat or place the pot of soup in a container with cold water.

•Transfer on food plastic containers, label and date and freeze.

SERVING INSTRUCTIONS:

•Allow the soup to thaw overnight in the refrigerator. Reheat over low heat.

•Before eating, add sour cream only on the amount you are going to eat.

NUTRITIONAL VALUE:

Calories	350
Carbs	13g
Fats	24g
Protein	24g

Ketogenic Freezer Short-Rib Stew

INGREDIENTS:

1 1/2 cup fresh cranberries
1 tbsp. finely shredded orange zest
1/2 cup brandy
1/2 cup dried cranberries
1/3 cup flour
2 tbsp. minced candied ginger
2 finely chopped medium onions
3 lbs. kabocha squash (1 small), seeded, peeled cut into 2-in. wedges
3 tbsp. Dutch-processed bittersweet cocoa powder
3 tbsps. vegetable oil, divided
4 minced garlic cloves
5 cup reduced-sodium beef broth
6 lbs. bone-in beef short ribs
About 1 tsp. black pepper
About 2 tsp. kosher salt, divided

INSTRUCTIONS:

•Pre-heat your oven to 500 degrees Fahrenheit. Use paper towels to wipe dry short ribs and sprinkle 1 tsp. each of pepper and salt. In an ovenproof pot, heat over med-high heat one Tbsp. of oil. In four batches, brown ribs and transfer to a bowl.

•Slice squash wedges crosswise, place on a baking sheet and add the rest of the oil. Roast for ten minutes until caramelized. Take it out of the oven and then lower the heat to 300 degrees Fahrenheit.

•Add onions and the rest of the salt to pot and set the heat at med-high stirring often, until it becomes soft, about three minutes. Add the flour and cook, stir until golden brown, about five minutes.

•Add in cocoa and garlic. Cook for one minute. Add in brandy and broth. Add ginger, cocoa, orange zest and dried cranberries and boil the mixture. Return the ribs to the pot, cover and then bake for 2 ½ hours.

•Take the pot out from the oven and remove the fat. Add in the kabocha and fresh cranberries. Cover and bake for around thirty mins. or until the kabocha becomes tender and the meat is pulling away from the bone.

FREEZING INSTRUCTIONS:

•Allow the soup to cool down. To speed up the cooling process, you can stir the soup to release the heat or place the pot of soup in a container with cold water.

•Transfer on food plastic containers, label and date and freeze.

SERVING INSTRUCTIONS:

•Allow the soup to thaw overnight in the refrigerator. Reheat over low heat.

NUTRITIONAL VALUE:

Calories   982
Carbs   31g
Fat   77 g
Protein   41 g

Ketogenic Freezer Broccoli Hamburger Casserole
Serves 4-6

INGREDIENTS
1 lb. ground beef
1/4 cup onion, chopped, 1 1/4 oz.
4 oz. can mushrooms, drained
16 oz. frozen broccoli
Salt and pepper, to taste

Sauce:
8 oz. sharp cheddar cheese, shredded
1/2 cup heavy cream
1/2 cup mayonnaise

INSTRUCTIONS

•Heat a skillet and slightly brown the onion, beef and mushrooms.
•Add seasonings and pour the fat out of the skillet.
•Place the frozen broccoli in a casserole with a cover.
•Pour 2 tbsps. of water, cover and heat in the microwave for 8 minutes on high.
•Ensure to stir until the broccoli is crisp and tender.
•Remove the broccoli and mix with beef mixture.
•Place all the sauce ingredients in a bowl and microwave for 2 minutes on high until smooth and melted.
•Continue to stir and once combined mix with the broccoli mixture.
• Adjust the seasonings once again.
•Bake at 350° for 20-25 minutes until the mixture becomes warm and bubbly.

FREEZING INSTRUCTIONS:

•Allow the mixture to cool well.
•Place the casserole a plastic container.
•Write down the date, label and leave in the freezer.

SERVING INSTRUCTIONS:

•Allow the mixture to thaw overnight in the refrigerator.
•Preheat in a microwave up to the required temperature.
•Serve and enjoy!

NUTRITIONAL VALUE:

Calories	760
Carbs	10g
Fat	65g
Protein	37g

Ketogenic Freezer Stuffed Beef Peppers
Serves 4

INGREDIENTS

2 large green peppers, halved lengthwise
1 lb. ground beef
1/4 cup onion, chopped,.
1 clove garlic, minced
1/2 cup tomato, chopped, about 2 oz.
Salt and pepper, to taste
4 oz. cheddar cheese, shredded
2 oz. cheddar cheese, shredded, for topping

INSTRUCTIONS

•Pour water into a large pot filling up-to mid-level and bring to a boil.
•Toss in the peppers and leave for 3-4 minutes.
•Drain the water.
•Slightly brown the onion, garlic and hamburger using the same pot.
•Remove the fat and toss in the tomatoes.
•Adjust seasonings as required.
•Cook the tomatoes for about 4 minutes and take out from the heat.
•Stir in the cheese (4oz).
•Place the peppers in a greased baking tray.
•Spread the meat on top and sprinkle a bit of cheese on the surface.
•Bake for 350F for 25 minutes

FREEZING INSTRUCTIONS:

•Allow the mixture to cool.
•Place in freezer bags, label with date and leave in the freezer.

SERVING INSTRUCTIONS:

•Thaw overnight in the refrigerator.
•Reheat up to the required temperature and serve.

NUTRITIONAL VALUE:

Calories	388
Carbs	6g
Fat	27g
Protein	30g

Ketogenic Freezer Cheesy Meatloaf
Serves 8

INGREDIENTS
2 lbs. ground beef
2 eggs
1/4 cup low carb ketchup
1 1/2 tsps. dry onion flakes
2 tsps. Seasoning Salt
1/4 tsp. pepper
4 oz. cheddar cheese, shredded
Glaze

Glaze:
1/2 cup low carb ketchup
1/4 tsp. dry mustard
2 Tbsps. granular Splenda

INSTRUCTIONS
•Place all the ingredients excluding the glaze in a bowl.
•Mix the ingredients until well combined.
•Line a loaf pan (9x5") using heavy duty foil.
•Press the meat mixture gently into the lined pan.
•Combine the ingredients for glaze and pour over the meat mixture.
•Bake for 15 minutes at 425F and then lower the temperature to 325F and leave for 50 minutes.

FREEZING INSTRUCTIONS:
•Leave the loaf for a few minutes to cool down.
•Cut into slices.
•Place in freezer bags, label with date and leave in the freezer.

SERVING INSTRUCTIONS:
•Thaw overnight in the refrigerator.
•Reheat in a microwave and serve and enjoy!

NUTRITIONAL VALUE

Calories   279
Carbs   3g
Fat   19g
Protein   24g

Ketogenic Freezer Chicken and Herb Parmesan
Serves 3

INGREDIENTS:
1/2 cup freshly grated parmesan cheese, 2 oz.
1 Tbsp. fresh parsley
1/2 tsp. basil
1/2 tsp. paprika
1/2 tsp. salt
1/4 tsp. pepper
Pinch garlic powder
3 boneless chicken breasts, pounded thin
1/4 cup butter
3 Tbsps. spaghetti sauce
3 oz. mozzarella cheese, shredded

INSTRUCTIONS:
•Combine the first few ingredients up to garlic powder and place in a shallow pan.
•Melt the butter and dip the thin chicken pieces in the melted butter.
•Coat the meat pieces with grated parmesan cheese.
•Place the coated meat in a baking tray.
•Bake for 20 minutes at 350F until the meat is cooked.
•Sprinkle 1 tbsp. of the spaghetti sauce and 1 oz. of the mozzarella cheese on top.
•Place the tray once again in the oven for about 5 minutes until the cheese becomes bubbly and completely melted.

FREEZING INSTRUCTIONS:
•Allow the mixture to cool down at room temperature.
•Place it in a plastic food storage container and don't forget to date and label.

SERVING INSTRUCTIONS:
•Remove from the freezer and let it thaw in the fridge overnight.

•Transfer into a baking tray and reheat until warm.

NUTRITIONAL VALUE

Calories   456
Carbs   3
Fat   30
Protein   42

Ketogenic Freezer Chicken with Peanut Curry Sauce

Serves 4

INGREDIENTS

2 Tbsps. oil
1 1/2 lbs. boneless chicken breast, cubed
Salt and pepper, to taste
8 oz. frozen cut green beans, thawed
8 oz. frozen bell pepper strips, thawed

Sauce:
13.5 oz. coconut milk (1 can)
1/2 cup chicken broth
1 Tbsp. red Thai curry paste
1/3 cup natural peanut butter
2 Tbsp. granular Splenda or equivalent liquid Splenda
1 Tbsp. lime juice
Cilantro for garnish, optional

INSTRUCTIONS

•Place the sauce ingredients excluding the cilantro in a 4 cup measuring cup.
•Whisk the ingredients and leave aside.
•Pour the oil into a skillet and allow to heat.
•Toss in the chicken and allow to sauté until the outer appearance turns opaque.
•Mix the peppers and green beans and leave for another 4 minutes ensuring to stir frequently.
•Pour the sauce into the meat mixture and allow to boil.
•Allow to simmer for about 7-8 minutes until the mixture becomes slightly thick in consistency.

FREEZING INSTRUCTIONS:

•Allow the mixture to cool down at room temperature.

•Place it in a plastic food storage container and don't forget to date and label.

SERVING INSTRUCTIONS:

•Remove from the freezer and let it thaw in the fridge overnight.
•Transfer into a skillet and reheat until warm.
•Serve with cilantro sprinkled on top.

NUTRITIONAL VALUE

Calories   608
Carbs   16g
Fat   38
Protein   48

Ketogenic Freezer Baked Meatballs

Yield 20-30 meatballs

INGREDIENTS

1 lb. ground beef
1 lb. bulk Italian sausage
2 tsps. dry minced onion
1/2 tsp. garlic powder
1/2 cup parmesan cheese, 2 oz.
2 eggs
1/2 tsp. salt
1/4 tsp. pepper

INSTRUCTIONS

•Place all the ingredients in a bowl.
•Mix the ingredients using your fingers until well combined.
•Shape the mixture into the shape of small golf balls.
•Spread the meat balls on a baking sheet which has sides.
•Bake for 20 minutes until the meatballs are fully done.
•Place in a colander and remove any excess egg and cheese remnants.

FREEZING INSTRUCTIONS:

•Allow the meatballs to cool down and place in freezer bags.
•Write the date and label the bags.

SERVING INSTRUCTIONS:

•Remove from the freezer and let it thaw in the fridge overnight.
•Transfer into a baking tray and reheat until warm.

NUTRITIONAL VALUE

Calories	92
Carbs	A trace
Fat	7g
Protein	6g

Conclusion

Thank you again for purchasing this book!

I hope this book was able to help you discover some amazing Ketogenic Diet Recipes. The next step is to get cooking!!!

FREE Gift - Keto Holiday Recipes
As a "thank you" for purchasing this book, I want to give you a gift absolutely 100% Free

go to http://freebookbonus.com/keto-recipes/

CPSIA information can be obtained
at www.ICGtesting.com
Printed in the USA
LVOW13s0252280218
568166LV00020B/946/P